BUILD
THE DAMN
THING
NOW

A SMALL BUSINESS OWNER'S GUIDE
TO FINALLY BECOMING MORE

TIFFANY LARGIE

DO THE
DAMN
THING™

DO THE
DAMN
THING™

Build the Damn Thing Now: A Small Business
Owner's Guide To Finally Becoming More

Copyright © 2022 by Tiffany Largie

Edited by: Jayda M. Largie

ISBN: 979-8-9865258-0-8

Printed in the United States of America

To my haters and naysayers who often told me that it was impossible, I was thinking too big and I would never make it... thanks for fueling my determination.

To my parents, Luvon and Winston, the immigrants that sacrificed so that I could be more. Without you, none of this is possible, look at the impact you have made on the world.

To my amazing family—Jayda, Maya, Kayla and El— thank you for keeping me, believing and filling in my gaps when I got weak until I could get right here.
–December 5, 2008

To the DO DAMN THING NATION: We have officially DONE THE DAMN THING. Thank you for choosing me, and thank you for teaching me the true POWER OF STORY.

CONTENTS

BUILD
THE DAMN
THING
NOW

INTRODUCTION

PEOPLE START A BUSINESS for many reasons. Some for passions, interests, and hobbies, others because they are simply tired of not having options in their current situations. However, all share a common interest and need—money.

Some of these businesses will grow a little, maybe able to scale a bit, but unfortunately quite a bit of them will plateau, eventually greeting death. They've plateaued because they can't understand why there is no more growth and don't know how to change it, or they are simply running a non-profitable company that could be better classified as a not-for-profit. The toughest spot for any business to be stuck in is both areas at the exact same time.

A business is like any living thing. When it stops growing, it appears to be sustaining itself for a period of time by using its reserves. However, quickly those reserves can turn into fumes and then death is around the corner. The business dies and then sometimes spiritually the owner does too. Then all the things related to that business start to die as well. This is an even bigger problem than the business itself facing death.

SMALL BUSINESSES DIE FOR THESE TEN REASONS:

1. They have no plan to dominate in their industry.
2. They are trapped from fear of failure.
3. They never do the research to understand their market well enough to get there.
4. They don't have marketing skills and do nothing to develop them.
5. They don't have any sales skills and don't develop them.
6. They are not willing to do whatever it takes.
7. They don't have the confidence in themselves to make it happen.
8. They don't build fans of their customers.
9. They don't hire or don't fire fast enough.
10. They try to do as much as they can themselves to "save money".

Small businesses don't grow and therefore don't make enough money because their owners simply think too small. Small thinking leads to small money. It is those few businesses who refuse to think small and focus on making BOSS MOVES ONLY that have the potential to become big and make big money and, as a result, build a big life. But what does it mean to think big or dream big? It means forcing your mind into an unfamiliar place to come up with unlimited possibilities and potential.

At some point you've heard the phrase, "You can be anything you want to be" or "You can do anything you put your mind to." Most dismiss the clichés, but a few listen. Like many, when I heard these I thought it was being said to give me hope or something else to believe in. I didn't think it was true. To be honest with you, those words meant nothing to me.

When I worked my 9-5, I had no freedom. I grew tired of asking permission from an employer to stay home and rest when I was ill. I didn't want to beg to take off time to stay home and look after my kid who had the flu. Not to mention, being broke was just no fun. I refused to live life on someone else's terms other than my own.

Starting a business was the only solution to my problems—all of them; money for me was the answer. Money for me was freedom, and freedom for me brought my happiness. I faced business death more than once in this critical time. At first I thought it was the products, then the customers, but ultimately—it was me. I was thinking too small.

Once I decided to change the way I think, I was able to own it, and control my business and dare myself to Dream and Think Big. I started to make the money I wanted instead of just the money I needed. Remember that third phrase you heard as a kid: "Money doesn't equal happiness?" Well, that's a lie. Money equals freedom, and freedom equals happiness. So therefore, money equals happiness. Your business is your road to freedom. I wrote this book for you, the awesome business owner who has a business and knows they are stuck and don't know how to break free. Either you can't figure out how to grow any more revenue, or you're running a business that is simply not profitable. This book is also for those who are just making enough money in their business to get by or rather to "take care of the bills." No one should be starting a business to "just pay their bills"—if that's what you want, then honestly, you should get a 9-5 job. In most scenarios it would be easier.

This book will show you how to up your business game quickly, so that you can start building a business you love and are excited about again. I know first hand if we can get this business thing right, we begin to change the course of everything else that's connected to us. Relationships, health, happiness, our own value, and our impact; impact on ourselves first, and then our impact on the world; they all get better. With more money you have more options, and more importantly you will build a solid foundation that can support you and fund your deepest desires. The first step is changing the way you think. Why? So that you can become someone really worth following.

ONE
THE PROBLEM AT LARGE

*"You're either doing the damn thing or
you're not. There is no in between."*

–Tiffany Largie

Back in 2013, American Express did a study that just blew my mind. The study revealed that the average small business owner right now in America took home an average annual salary of just $68,000 in their small business. Whoa! That's scary. In my opinion, small business owners should strive to make $1,000,000 a year at minimum. For the cost of what it takes to be in business after paying for taxes, tools, resources, and people, making under $100,000 means you have an expensive hobby. Unfortunately, it's true. Yes, you have to start out somewhere, but it is vital to set your ambitions high enough to pay for the dreams you have and the lifestyle you want. If you decide that you are building a 2 million dollar company, you'll get there. Question is, why didn't you decide on more than that amount. Take a moment with me and say out loud the number you thought you would hit in your small business this year. Why did you choose that number? Have you actually decided what kind of company you were going to be? Or did you start this year with a "hope and pray strategy" that maybe you'd hit a number higher than last year? What would happen if you decided that you were going to be a 15 million dollar company? The real question is, why haven't you decided that you are going to be a 15 million dollar business owner? Is it really that impossible? Has anyone confirmed to you that you can't do it? OR have you told yourself that you can't do it?

I want you to entertain the idea that you may not be where you want to be because you have not declared where you want to be. Now let's get back to this study. The real kicker for me from this study was the second half of the findings which stated that of those statistics, fifteen percent of these small business owners had to get a second job just to make ends meet and cover their bills at home! This made me sick.

Life is just too damn short for anyone to spend time running a business so that to the eye it looks "good," but behind the scenes the CEO is not far from broke. They hold onto the current state of the business for the sake of public perception on employee size, building size, or the length of years even though the company is not profitable. Because it allows them to hide other areas of their life such as management style or inability to gain control of a department; it seems like a good idea. Real talk, though: it's really a terrible plan.

A small business, according to the Small Business Administration, is one with fewer than 500 employees. In the U.S. today, there are 32 million small businesses in operation, and roughly 1.5 million jobs are created by these businesses annually. That's a huge impact!

Here are some realities about these 32 million small businesses according to fundera.com:

- **86.3 percent of small business owners make less than $100,000 a year in income.**
- **82 percent of the businesses that fail mention a lack of cash flow as the sole factor in their collapse.**
- **Of all firms in the U.S., 99.9 percent of them are small businesses.**
- **19.9 percent of businesses are woman owned.**

- **44 percent of all U.S. economic activity belongs to small businesses.**
- **Less than 7 percent of all small businesses get to 3 percent figures and**
- **Less than 12 percent get to six figures.**

(I wanted us to have a super quick snapshot of where we are together in small business at this time, AND I wanted to make sure that you understood how much of an impact you have in the economy. Baby, it's HUGE!)

Did you do the math yet? This means that almost 90 percent of small businesses in America see less than six figures in revenue.

Is that you? Are you in the 90 percent or the 10 percent of all business owners? If you have been in business for more than two years and are not doing six figures in revenue yet, I might be personally concerned. There's nothing wrong with having a small hustle or business to supplement your income, but too many entrepreneurs sell themselves short on what they are capable of achieving. The reason why you are not making the money you want or growing at the rate you imagined is not because you're not smart, or because you don't have a great product, or a unique skill to offer the world. The reason why you're not making the money at this point is because you're thinking too small. I know that you didn't start a business to work crazy hours and still try to make ends meet. Not making enough money in your small business is not just a problem when it comes to paying your bills. It becomes a problem in multiple areas of your life including your health, your relationships with your friends, family, spouse, or kids, as well as your overall happiness. Amazingly, out of all of our entire current workforce, nearly half of workers are employed by a small business. This is great! Still, unfortunately, small businesses are closing their doors at staggering rates every day. Out of every ten businesses, only seven survive in year one. From that, half of those survive five years, a third survive ten years, and a quarter survive up to fifteen years.

Scary.

They are not closing their doors because they want to.

They close them because they have to. They close them because they are out of money and totally out of options.

BEING WITHOUT OPTIONS SUCKS

ABOUT TWENTY YEARS AGO I was living in Miami, Florida, frustrated as hell, all the time. To be quite honest with you, the majority of every week I just wanted to die. I didn't have the answers I needed, I didn't know where to look for the answers, and I felt like I was in a losing world where there was no way for me to win.

I was in a marriage where my husband was gone all of the time. He was in the streets; there was always drugs. When he was home, he had these episodes that would often end in a broken door, a broken window, broken glass, and sometimes blood. In addition to that, I had two daughters, Jayda and Maya, twenty-two months apart whom I loved very much. As much as I loved them, the truth is I could not figure out how to change our circumstances. I wanted to leave so many times and just start a new life for us, but I couldn't. I couldn't because I didn't have money, I didn't have a college education, and I didn't have any degrees to fall back upon. At that time, everyone I knew told me to go back to school, to go get a license or some type of certification. After I acquired those items, there was this notion that I would be more valuable, would be capable of making more money, and I would have a resource to change my financial circumstances (a.k.a. my options). What I didn't know at the time—or rather, what I didn't hear from anyone—was that all of those ideas I was being pointed towards were outside of myself.

There came a time when I would just look at the sky and say, "Well…why can't this version of me be enough?" That's really the question at hand: Why can't the version that I have right now be enough? Why do I have to acquire a license or certification to be valuable? That notion just felt stupid. I mean, what if I never got any of those things? Would I never be valuable? No. I knew there had to be a different way. The moment I made a decision to stop thinking small, specifically when it came to myself in my story, my life, my capacity, that's when everything changed. I got the courage to start my very first business, and more importantly, I had the momentum, the clarity, and desire to protect my mental state. It helped me understand that it wasn't about me making more money, it was about me being more.

I don't know where you are right now in life, but I do know that the universe at this exact moment is calling you to be more. Whoa! Did I just bring in the word "universe"? Yes, yes, I did. But first things first: your tolerations…get rid of them. Tolerations are the enemy. The way we do one thing is ultimately the way we do all the things. Who and what are you tolerating right now?

When I began my journey in making money I started—wait a minute. Tiffany, is this some blue-book talking about the universe, energy, and spirituality?

Nope.

The root of all of my problems really came down to the fact that I didn't know I could become more. I let my tolerations stunt my growth. My lack of a decision to become more kept me in a marriage for six years. I was frustrated most of the time and alone in an apartment where the rent was past due. If not that, then I was on my way to an infection because I couldn't afford to get medical treatment. On top of that, there was often little to no food in the fridge and I did not have a car.

- **I was tolerating my circumstances.**
- **I was tolerating how I was being treated.**
- **I was tolerating the way my husband treated our marriage.**
- **I was tolerating him being in the streets.**

- **I was tolerating drug usage around me.**
- **I was tolerating the fact that sometimes I was in the middle of a broken door, a broken wall, a broken item, or something was currently being slammed.**
- **I tolerated that behavior around me, which meant I accepted it.**

Those tolerations kept me trapped physically, spiritually, mentally, and ultimately financially. When we are trapped, it's really hard to grow. Which is why during this time I didn't. Everything around me stayed the same. Because I was tolerating the behavior I was conditioned to accept the circumstances as a norm. Me making a decision to stop tolerating the behavior was the first step in me becoming the kind of person that was worth following. We will identify that as becoming the CEO of Tiffany Largie; a CEO worth following. The first followers I had on my team were my babies, Jayda and Maya.

Do the closest people around you actually follow you? I want you to think of yourself as a company. Stay with me for a moment. You yourself are a business. You have a company culture, a customer service department, a sales department, and every time you go shopping for clothes or style your hair, it is like a personal marketing department. Letting go of tolerations was the key to me making the first move in becoming the kind of CEO over the years that starts to win. From my first CEO position I went on to build many multiple six-figure businesses and then I went on to build multiple seven-figure ones. My business partners were companies like Xerox Corporation, HP, Franco Postalia and Great America. In 2014, I was running a multiple, seven-figure business and I knew it was time for me to sell so I could build something new.

For almost a decade since then I have constantly sought the greatest versions of myself and have used them to become the kind of CEO that is worth following. This book is going to give you a roadmap for changing your entire game, brick-by-brick, department by department, and layer-by-layer so that you can actually build the kind of business you want, and so that you can build the kind of life that you were meant to have.

I was being called to be more as a woman, but more importantly I was being called to be more as a human. Little did I know that this requirement of being more would be the key thing that I needed in my back pocket to become the kind of CEO that other people wanted to work for and eventually build the kind of teams that are willing to give me 200 percent without me having the means to match those dollars at the time.

Small thinking is at the core of everything we do in business that eventually leads to lack of money for the small business owner.

The truth is that you may just be thinking too small in your potential and in how you conduct your company. With my clients, I find that commonly they come in thinking too small, specifically when it comes to areas such as marketing, sales, and operations. Even if you don't undergo a formal business education, it's incumbent upon you to educate yourself on all aspects of running a company. You might consider looking at alternative options to brush up on these concepts online or even at your local library. There are plenty of resources at your fingertips if you just take the time to identify them.

Listen, if making six and seven figures in business is possible for some, such as the 10 percent, then it's possible for all. If you are on the brink of closing your doors or asking yourself every other week if it's even worth it…understand, it's not a should, it's a must to think bigger. It's a must for your health, for your dreams, and for the future of your family—not to mention your sanity.

NEXT

So let's get real. What kind of revenue are you generating in your business? Are you in the 90 percent, or 10 percent, or 2 percent? Knowing where you are right now is the most important part of building our tomorrows, all of them. Now crunch the numbers:

1. What is your current revenue?

2. What was your revenue last year?

3. What is your target revenue this year?

4. How much money did you take home last year?

5. How much money will you take home this year?

6. What prevents you from making more money?

7. What things in your personal life are suffering from lack of money?

8. What would you do this year with an extra $250,000 in income?

TWO
STOP BEING PART OF THE PROBLEM

"You have to be willing to fail 97 percent
of the time to succeed."

–Tiffany Largie

I T WAS A BEAUTIFUL, bright sunny day. I was sitting at a gorgeous resort with an amazing pool—you know the one that just begs you to come in. When you're near it, you feel like it's calling your name. To the left of me there were beautifully hidden caves and a waterfall. On my right, palm trees swaying with the breeze.

Working for yourself means that it can be hard to sneak away for vacations. That time away relaxing is one of the rare times when you aren't hustling and building, but it's important to set time for yourself to take a break now and then to refocus. And I had definitely earned this break!

Everyone was playing and having a good time in the water. Young and old. Everyone, except one kid who just kept walking around attempting to play with everyone from the outside. Every so often, someone said, "Come on, jump in!" He didn't. It must have been about an hour and a half that I watched this kid walk around and around. Wanting to try the water but clearly afraid of what, for him, at that time, was the unknown. A few times he did get pretty close, but just when he looked like he was about to jump, I saw him go motionless; he was plagued with fright.

The truth is, he didn't go in because he was afraid. His fear kept him trapped right outside of the pool. Everyone else was already in the water. He was the only one who could let himself out of this cage. It was sad. Contemplating is over! Then one of his buddies got out, came from behind, and pushed him in! Within seconds he discovered what he had been missing out on big time. Within seconds he was having TONS of fun…what was he afraid of in the first place?

There was no way to know what it would actually be like until he got in. So why did he wait so long? This is a lot like being in business. We make moves that we are certain of.

Thinking small provides security. There are minimal risks involved for small thinkers. Small moves provide predictable outcomes. This makes the next move safe. For this reason alone, small thinking is common for small business owners. I believe that small thinking is common for people in general. They choose to think small simply because it's safer. No one wins the lotto by playing it safe.

GOOD BUDDIES

FEAR IS DEFINED BY Webster's dictionary as "An unpleasant emotion caused by the belief that someone or something is dangerous, likely to cause pain, or a threat." Seriously, who wants to be anywhere that presents danger, threat, or pain? Humans go out of their way to avoid it, unfortunately in doing so we often miss all the opportunities being laid out for us to stretch, grow, and elevate our game to get to the next level.

Fear never hangs out alone; it has some good buddies that always hang close by. The usual suspects are always close: doubt, concern, and anxiety. Recognize any of them? Felt them lately? They are right around the corner when there are important moves that you need to make happen, like let-ting go of your tolerations…they are notorious and consistent when they show up, especially when you're trying to make a decision in your business. Remember, you are the boss; they can't win. You can't afford for them to win.

We have choices to make here. Even if we do nothing, we technically made a choice. Surely these kinds of questions produce anxiety, concern, or plain ole fear, especially when considering things like:

- **Who to hire?**
- **How much should we pay them?**
- **Can we really handle that project?**
- **Can I afford that?**
- **Should you really expand?**
- **If so, when's the right time…will there ever be a right time?**
- **What if they don't like the proposal?**
- **How much is that going to cost?**
- **What am I going to do if it doesn't work out?**

These are just some of the critical areas in your business that either promote growth or prohibit it. If you're not making choices in these areas, your business becomes stifled.

I know you don't like to make choices. You may provide me many explana-tions as to why, but all reasons come back to the fear of failure. In business, you just can't be afraid to fail, or get it wrong. Failure is part of the deal when you sign up for entrepreneurship. If you don't fail, you can't learn. If you don't learn, it's virtually impossible to grow. You can't let fear in, not even an inch. Fear is always waiting outside the door; it's around every corner.

THE EFFECTS OF FEAR—YOU DEVALUE YOURSELF

FEAR FEEDS STRAIGHT OFF of self-doubt. It works hard day and night to devalue you, your product, and your service. It forces you to play small in your field and win small, if at all. An opportunity will come along and you'll entertain seizing it for a moment. However, once you really look at the scope of it, you convince yourself that it's just way too big of a request and your small company wouldn't be considered anyway, so what's the use?

You're dead wrong. The truth is that your small business can often offer a more tailored solution than a large corporation. Your potential customer didn't want a large corporation; they wanted you. You were exactly what they were looking for, but you didn't participate. So you weren't even considered. You'll go after small customers that you feel safer with—ones you're certain you can handle, smaller opportunities where you feel more prepared to support. Sound familiar? Small opportunities often result in small money; you're constantly forced to find new customers and produce new small sales. Playing small forces you to work cheap! If you're a non-profit, then that's a different story—although I would keep in mind that even non-profit leaders need to have a strong sense of how to keep revenue flowing and how to run a financially solvent enterprise. Chances are strong that if you're reading this book, you're a for-profit business looking to make bigger profits in your company.

YOU KEEP YOUR DREAMS SMALL

So we took some time to meet some good buddies of fear, but everyone has a best buddy. Fear has one too. Let me introduce you to uncertainty. If there's one thing that's clear about uncertainty, it is that it absolutely hates big thinkers and dreamers. Uncertainty creates that physical feeling of sheer panic that makes you either doubt the possibility of something, or deem it flat out ridiculous because you can't see how it will happen, just like the boy at the edge of the pool. Big thinking dismisses uncertainty as not being credible and moves forward with no more thought of what is or isn't possible. It's simple: if we can think it or dream it, then it's possible. You'll go and grow nowhere by keeping the possibilities in a small box. Big thinkers dream. They dream frequently. Don't get me wrong—they don't just daydream. They start to build as they imagine their dream and along the way, they add more colors and detail to the map to get to it. The how comes after they get started, not before.

You may be one of the ones that dream, but do you dream and then immediately try to figure out the how? Those who try to figure out how to first stay small thinkers, and they don't mature into big thinkers, because once that how comes into question, the dream becomes fuzzy. Often with big ideas, the how is not clear. Most of the time there is no one way or predictable avenue available when dreaming. This is what makes it a dream in the first place. The how is irrelevant if we have a what and a why. If we are clear on how to get to the destination, then it's not a dream, it's a thought, and, unfortunately, it has no growth options available for you. You won't have to stretch to get there. If you don't stretch in your business to reach that dream, you're playing it safe and thinking small.

YOU DON'T GROW

FEAR IS LIKE A CAGE. It traps you indefinitely. Most living things can't grow in cages. You've got to get out and grow. If your business doesn't grow, your finances don't grow. If they don't grow, you don't grow. Your opportunities and experiences are limited when you're trapped in fear. We don't want that. You didn't take on the risk of entrepreneurship to make the same amount of money as your middle-class neighbor working a 9-5 job. Like any part of nature, if you don't grow, eventually you'll die. Trust me; if you stay in that cage long enough, fear finds a way to come over all the time. Instead of giving you some notice like it does at first, fear and its friends will just start dropping in whenever they feel like it. All hours of the day! When you're with your friends, or when you're with your family. You may be thinking, *This doesn't apply to me; my business is large enough to be exempt from fear.* But let me tell you: no one is exempt. Kmart, RadioShack, Borders, Blockbuster, Waldenbooks: all of these thought they were exempt too. Even the most successful of enterprises just can't afford to be complacent. If you aren't keeping your finger on the pulse of how technology and the market are changing, you run the risk of being left behind in the dust eventually.

You can't be left behind in the dust. That just don't make no damn sense; you didn't start this thing to not win. We started it to win; so, let's win.

ARCHENEMIES

BY NO MEANS AM I telling you that it is wrong to be afraid. Being the leader and owning a business can be scary…you're making new moves day by day and the consequences are not always clear. You're constantly being challenged to get stronger, and somehow becoming stronger is scary. Trust me; I totally get it. My problem is not with you being afraid; it's what you do with fear when it comes knocking on the door of your mind that changes the game.

Fear gets creative sometimes and disguises itself. We know we need to make a decision, but then become caught up with do-I-or-don't-I? What happens here is that logic and rational reason come up. Again, you don't choose either. After all, you have good reasons to not try it, right? Wrong. Coming up with a justified reason still places you back at square one. Trapped. Just because you have a fancy excuse now, doesn't make it any better.

If there is one thing that fear hates, it is movement. Let me repeat this: fear hates movement! It doesn't like movement at all. Movement is definitely an archenemy of fear. You know why? Because movement of any kind forces new and bigger thoughts. Movement gives you confidence and makes you feel that the impossible is possible…fear doesn't want that. To grow, you have to move. You have to try new things.

GET OUT OF THE COMFORT ZONE!

DON'T BE A VICTIM OF FEAR. Don't be part of the society of small thinkers. There is nothing in the land of fear; people who live in that land are often broke, frustrated, and live with limitations.

You already have all the tools you need to absolutely kick ass in your business. You have everything you need to qualify as a big thinker. To grow you have to take risks. You were meant to win in your business. I am sure of it. But, I'm not talking about a series of small victories. I am talking slam dunk… massive wins. Wins that will surely put you in control of your business and, more importantly, in your life. Whatever decisions you haven't made yet because you were afraid, make them now. Right now.

Think and Grow Rich by Napoleon Hill puts it best in one of my absolute favorite stories of one of history's Spanish conquistadors, Hernán Cortés:

> *A long while ago, a great warrior faced a situation which made it necessary for him to make a decision which ensured his success on the battlefield. He was about to send his armies against a powerful foe, whose men outnumbered his own. He loaded his soldiers into boats, sailed to the enemy's country, unloaded soldiers and equipment, and then gave the order to burn the ships that had carried them. Addressing his men before the first battle, he said, "You see the boats going up in smoke. That means that we cannot leave these shores alive unless we win! We now have no choice—we win, or we perish!" They won!*

Every person who wins in any undertaking must be willing to burn his ships and cut all sources of retreat. This is truly the only real way to face fear. Only by doing so can one be sure of maintaining that state of mind known as a burning desire to win, which is essential to success.

Do you have a security boat that you are holding on to? If so, it's time to burn the whole damn thing, the bridge of whatever is keeping you comfortable and safe!

THOUGHT OPPORTUNITY

NAME FIVE FEARLESS PEOPLE that you admire. They don't necessarily need to be famous or business leaders.

1.

2.

3.

4.

5.

Why do you admire each one?

1.

2.

3.

4.

5.

What one trait or habit can you adopt from each one? What's one that you can adopt right now?

GROWTH OPPORTUNITY

ALL RIGHT; LET'S FACE those fears. Let's start moving!

What decisions have you been reluctant to make or have been stalling on, but know you have to make them to grow and get to your next level?

1.

2.

3.

Why haven't you made them? What are you waiting for?

What choice could you make that would cause massive movement?

What is your greatest fear in your business?

What prospect haven't you tried to reach because you think you're not big enough?

THREE
APPLAUSE PLEASE; YOU ARE ON TIME.

"Money can't buy direct happiness, but it sure as hell is responsible for a lot of happy moments."

–TIFFANY LARGIE

As a kid, money was tight in my family, but my parents made it hard to notice. When the holiday season came around at the end of the year, my mom would start building the festivities and I was quick to embrace and push forward the holiday agenda. However, one particular winter was tough for our family because money was crazy tight. This Christmas, it was hard for my parents to hide it. December 15th came around and there was no wonderfully-smelling pine tree up like there usually was, and not a single present in sight. I remember hearing my parents argue much about money during that early December.

It was obvious that Christmas was in trouble. My mom had it written all over her face…you know what I'm talking about. The look. As an adult, you've had it before. I know as an adult, I definitely have. It's the "What the hell am I going to do?" look, which is a combination of anger, frustration, worry, disappointment, and despair mixed in with the slightest bit of desperation and embarrassment all at the same time.

At the age of nine, I had learned to recognize that face that often came when I asked questions related to money. Each year my mom would give me the "Big Book" that came in the mail late November from Toys"R"Us, in which I would circle all the things I dreamed of getting for Christmas. I did not get every item on my list; I only got some, but I usually had choices.

> *"Money can't buy happiness, but it sure as hell*
> *is responsible for a lot of happy moments."*
> –Tiffany Largie

A few months after Christmas, my birthday came around and I got a $20 bill in the mail from my grandmother tucked inside a beautiful card. I was so excited! I had never gotten a $20 bill before, all for myself. Like most kids at that time, twenty bucks was really a huge deal. I mean I was close to being rich at this point!

My parents told me to save it and that sounded…umm…boring.

I spent the following day and night trying to figure out what to spend it on. The anticipation was killing me. Truthfully this thing was just burning a hole through my pocket! I was sure of one thing though—I didn't want to just blow it.

This was a rare occasion, and whatever I did with it, I wanted it to be big. So instead of running to the store, I hid the twenty in my secret box I kept under my bed. I then thought and thought for what seemed like months, but in actuality it was only a few days short of a work week and then it happened! I knew what to do with my money.

CLARITY ON WHAT YOU WANT…AND WHY

IF THERE WAS ONE thing I knew for sure, it was that I wanted more money. That was a no-brainer. I came to the conclusion that I was going to start my own business. When I inquired a couple weeks prior, my parents had told me I was too young to get a job, so this was the next best thing.

I had always wanted to know what it would be like to have a hundred dollars. I figured that it would take me getting a $20 bill each year for five years to get to a hundred dollars!

Waiting until I turned fifteen to get to a hundred bucks seemed ridiculous; for a now ten-year-old, that was literally an eternity. Saving that money would have been right at the seat of small thinking. Saving it was safe, no risk involved. It would have been the easiest path, and it would take no planning with the result within reach.

I knew that I could do more with that twenty than just stick it under a mattress and save it. At this point, I had no idea how this was going to work. I just knew that I was going to start a business and make more than a hundred dollars doing it.

WHAT

I KNOW YOU'RE WONDERING what kind of business I started. Well, naturally I went into a field closest to me at the time. Something I had an interest in, knew much about, and had a clear clientele to sell it to. Yup! You guessed it: I started a candy business. It was the perfect fit; I had access to a prospective client base daily.

HOW

I WAS TEN. There were only so many options for me to get this product out.

Option 1...the safe option...I could have sold my candy door-to-door in my neighborhood. But I knew that I was limited in how many houses I could go to by myself and who may or may not be interested in buying candy, right?

There may not have been kids in each of those houses. I would have been wasting resources and time in areas where my target market didn't exist. This option had too many limitations and no risk and no real potential for growth.

Option 2…the risky option… Understanding the potential of my product at the time, I made an executive decision to take the candy hustle to the front door of where I was sure my customers would be each day. I went to the local pharmacy and spent all but two dollars and asked the cashier back for change in quarters (I had to be able to break a $1 bill after all). I was now going to be in business. When my parents caught me later that day filling up my backpack with candy getting ready on Monday, they didn't know what to say. My parents entertained my idea, and though they supported me, they were afraid. They were too focused on the what-ifs. There were risks. What if no one liked the candy I chose? Or, what if I got caught. Even though I was scared, I was too focused on the possibility of success in my business. I was already committed to my big thoughts and big dreams of earning a hundred dollars that year.

THE PLAN

EVERY STEP HAD TO be thought out; at first I was going to the store around the corner that I could walk to. But over a period of time, I found out that a local grocery store sold the same candy but for almost half the price!

It wasn't two weeks before a new routine had formed. I can recall just how excited I was waiting for my dad to wake up around five o'clock in the afternoon after school; he worked the night shift. At least fifteen minutes before he came downstairs, I would stand by the door with my shoes on ready to go to the store. I carried a list of exactly what I was going to buy and how much it would cost me. I didn't want to bring too much money—afraid I would lose it. The whole purchase was thought out, planned, and prepared. There was nothing more exciting at this time.

The five-minute car ride gave me enough time to think about where I would store my profits each day. I tried to guess what time of the day I would run out of candy: "Before lunch or after recess?" By my third week in business, I was selling out of candy every day! Do the math with me.

Each bag of candy cost $2.99 and I sold each candy for .25 cents a piece. My margins were close to fifty percent. That's a sweet book of business. Just like any business model…it started slow…I had to sell myself. Nothing came easy…but like all great business, at first it came slowly, then word got around, and by the end of the year, my little investment of twenty dollars to start my business became a whopping *$80 a week*. Listen, I was banking almost $320 a month at ten years old. I would have made it to the Forbes list of the Top Two Percent Wealthiest Fifth Graders. I can still remember my mom asking to borrow some money…it was great.

SUCCESS FACTORS

EVEN THOUGH I WAS scared, I was willing to take the risk. After all, I was determined to make those one hundred dollars. It became critical that I was able to visualize and specify the goal I was striving for. Whether you are working hard to be able to max out your Roth IRA, buy a new boat, or just take your family on vacation, it is critical that you have a specific target in mind. Having a "North Star" you are striving toward will help keep you motivated during the tough times.

One of the first steps in thinking big is knowing your maximum potential, even when no one else around you does. Second is knowing your product or service that you want to sell.

YOUR TURN

1. **What is it about your product that makes it unique in the market?**
2. **Can your product go beyond the markets you're currently serving?**
3. **Are you getting the money you deserve for your product?**

ACTIVITY

DO THE MATH. How much can you get for your product and what would it take?

There are only two ways to make more money with your current product. **We can increase or decrease either the quantity we sell OR the price.**

Let's see what happens when we increase the **quantity**:

WIDGET	PRICE	MONTHLY	ANNUAL
100	$20.00	$2,000	$24,000
120	$20.00	$2,400	$28,800
140	$20.00	$2,800	$33,600
180	$20.00	$3,600	$43,200

Now let's increase the **price**:

WIDGET	PRICE	MONTHLY	ANNUAL
100	$20.00	$2,000	$24,000
100	$28.00	$2,800	$33,600
100	$34.00	$3,400	$40,800
100	$39.00	$3,900	$46,800

Both models have value. However, in my opinion, it's easier to figure out how to sell more things to the same customer than it is to find more customers to sell them on a widget piece. Is your product worth more than you are asking for it? If you don't believe so as it is…what can you add on to this core to create more value in the offering? I'll give you some ideas in Chapter 12.

Now put in your actual numbers for your core products; **how many did you sell last month?**

WIDGET	PRICE	MONTHLY	ANNUAL

Now you try it with your actual numbers from last month. What happens if you **increase the quantity by, let's say, just 10 percent.**

WIDGET	PRICE	MONTHLY	ANNUAL

What would happen in your business if you **increased the price by 10 percent but kept all the quantities the same?**

WIDGET	PRICE	MONTHLY	ANNUAL

Did you discover some possibilities in your business? If so, what?

Which one are we going to focus on? Are we going to increase the price, or keep the price the same but make a slight difference in the quantity that we sell?

FOUR
THEY ARE ALL WRONG.
GET CREATIVE.

"Creativity is at the base of every big thinker."

−Tiffany Largie

HAD BEEN ON THE job for less than three months when I was diagnosed with a medical condition that landed me in the hospital. At the time I was making 10 bucks an hour as an administrative assistant in a large Fortune 500 corporation. It wasn't but two days into my stay at the hospital when I called my boss at work to let her know I had been admitted to the hospital. She told me she was sorry to hear I was in the hospital and then told me she needed to transfer me to the HR department. Minutes later, a woman whom I didn't know got on the phone and said hello.

I began to tell her about my ordeal of being at the hospital and that I anticipated to be out in a few days and would surely be back to work the next week.

She paused for a moment. Then the conversation went like this:

HR Lady: Tiffany, that's unfortunate. But company policy states that you must be back on the third day. Which means that you're expected to be back tomorrow morning.

ME: That's impossible. I don't think I'll be discharged for a few more days at least! What am I supposed to do?

HR Lady: I can't tell you what you're supposed to do.

ME: Don't I have sick days or something?

HR Lady: You have not been here long enough to have accumulated sick days.

ME: What do I do now?

HR Lady: Again, Tiffany, I can't tell you that, but I can tell you that you need to be here first thing tomorrow morning.

ME: What happens if I don't show up?

HR Lady: You forfeit your job.

ME: What?! But that's not fair.

HR Lady: Well, it's not about what's fair. It's about following the rules.

I was soooooo heated at this point. I was literally fuming.

HR Lady: So, Tiffany, what do you plan on doing?

This last question just hit me the wrong way and I responded.

ME: I will be sending someone to collect my things in the morning. Thanks.

I was so done with that chick. I hung up the phone. It was a scary moment. But in retrospect, it was one of the best things that ever happened to me.

LESSON: DON'T QUIT WHEN YOU'RE MAD WITHOUT A BACKUP PLAN.

I WAS MAD AND rightfully so, but now I was also voluntarily jobless. I let my anger totally stand in the way of good sense. I was a single parent with another child on the way. I had bills due and I had to make a decision. Of course I could have gone to look for another job, but honestly I was already tired of being told what to do and when. I didn't like the feeling of having to ask permission to be sick! For me that just seemed ridiculous. I was done with working for someone else.

So I made a decision that I would start a business. There were two factors I had to consider with this option: I needed a business that I could start from home, and I only had $140 or so that I could save from my last pay-check which would come at the end of that week. Shortly after leaving the hospital and getting back home, I started to research what business I could start. I nailed down the top 50 businesses that could be started at home and focused on them. Looking for the lowest-cost option with the greatest potential, I decided to start a gift basket company. As a young mom with two kids, that was a tough thing to do.

At this point I had nothing to lose and figured it had to be easier working for myself than for someone else. It had to work; being an entrepreneur was the only way out of my situation.

The absolute most important thing I learned was that when everything goes astray, you have to do what it takes to make it work.

And so that's what I did. I made that business work—I had a successful gift basket business.

LESSON: BE WILLING TO DO WHATEVER IT TAKES

I REALLY BEGAN TO own that lesson even more when I was running my gift basket business. I was doing okay, but definitely not making enough to put any money away. I was making just *enough* and I surely wasn't having any fun in the process. I'll tell you right now, I absolutely hated baskets.

One day I was at the park playing with my kids and I saw all of these trucks across the street by a ballroom. Wondering why there was so much activity I walked over to find out.

When I crossed the street, I saw that all of the trucks represented different companies. One looked like it was from a local bakery, one was from a florist, and the other was stacked high with tables and chairs. This place was hopping!

I maneuvered past the trucks because now I wanted to take a peek inside. I saw a woman who was in the center of a large room shouting out instructions to different sets of teams in different parts of the room. As far as I was concerned, it looked like there was a party going on and I like a party as much as anyone. So here she was throwing the party, possibly the ultimate party.

THE PITCH

IT WAS CLEAR THAT she was in charge of running the show. I wondered what her business really was at this point. I walked up to her, introduced myself, and asked her what she did.

She responded with, "I put on events." I said, "Events?" I was a little confused.

She chimed in, "Weddings, anniversaries, galas, meetings, and things like that."

Oh man. The wheels in my head were turning quick. In my mind I was thinking, *I would like to be in this business*; it looked like fun.

You're probably thinking that I was nuts, but think about it. Buying her business would be easier since I knew nothing about the industry. It would give me the ability to take my amateur knowledge of business and move it into a business that was already up and running. I was going to buy a business, not start one from scratch. I didn't have the money, BUT I saw an opportunity and I wanted more. I knew I was capable of more. I was.

Let me remind you that I absolutely hated baskets. This seemed like a fun alternative.

So without plans and without thinking, I said to her, "I am always on the lookout for opportunities—what do you think about selling me your business?"

She paused and looked at me for a long time. She asked me if I was serious. I told her, "Yes, I am serious. Dead serious." Not to mention a little scared, but I was very serious.

She then responded, "I am busy right now, so it's not a good time," but she handed me her card and told me to call her in a week. My jaw dropped. I didn't show it, of course, but the "inside me" surely dropped my jaw.

I did my homework on her business that week. She had a little store front right off of a major road on the east side of town and out of that shop she appeared to offer just about everything that you can imagine pertaining to event planning.

In a week I met with her. When we met, she told me that she had actually been thinking about selling and she wanted $25,000 for the business. I thought to myself, *That's not that much money*—but when you don't have $25,000, it turns out that's a whole lot of money. So I told her that I thought that it sounded like a fair price, which is just funny, because I had no clue what a fair price even was. One, because I had never bought a business, and two, because I had no money! Let me just tell you what happened next.

I said, "So, here's the deal. Sell me the business and carry the note and I will pay you $30,000 for the business. That's $5,000 for six months."

A few weeks later she had an attorney draw up the papers. I went to a law office and we had a signing. I signed the papers with her and her lawyer at the table. I had officially closed on my first business. I was an owner of a new brick and mortar business? Well, I thought so.

Let me start this next section with some context.

I was young. I didn't have the money to hire an attorney and was too naive to ask many questions or do any real research. Because I didn't have any money, and she seemed nice, I thought she was doing me a favor...giving me a leg up in life and providing me with an opportunity.

The agreement was that I would take all the new customers and she would keep her existing ones. Perfect, right? This business had a phone and a website that I had seen, and signs on the front door. Plus, she had been doing business in this location in Miami for well over six years, which meant instant walk-in traffic. This would be a walk-in-the-park for me. In the business I had owned before, I always had to go out and find my customers. At this point, I felt like I had learned a thing or two about business in general and was ready. I had taken the time to learn more about what it takes to run a business. My learning however was not rooted solely in reading or classes, but in real-world experience. My knowledge had grown, my confidence was strong, and I set my sights high. This was definitely way bigger than my little basket business. In my mind, a bigger business meant more money. I needed to make more money; I was desperate. I could not pay my bills, these kids were getting more expensive to take care of, and their dad was still nowhere to be found.

I really just wanted more options in life, and more options came with money. I had to make this happen.

NAYSAYERS COME IN ALL FORMS

I WILL NEVER FORGET those early conversations with my family and friends. They wanted to carry me off to the looney bin. I made the move before I told them about it, specifically for this reason. I sensed that they would attempt to discourage me from what I knew I was capable of, not to mention I had already made up my mind. I had no money, and no experience, and I just signed a note for 30K to buy a business, but I was confident. It didn't matter what they thought. It mattered what I thought.

Remember, you have to believe in you first before you can expect anyone else to believe in you.

They didn't believe I would succeed because they were small thinkers who were trying to limit what was possible. Every last one of them had a 9-5 job and made a fixed amount of money every month no matter how hard they worked. I had created an opportunity for myself, which allowed me to make any amount that I wanted. If I worked harder or extra, I got paid for it. I let those small thinkers stay in their 9-5 world, while I had an opportunity to write my own paycheck. I was set.

By refusing to think small when presented with an opportunity, I bought a business at an early age. I may not have been ready for it, but when are you ever "ready" to BUILD THE DAMN THING? The truth is that sometimes in life, you simply need to take the plunge. You can never be fully prepared or have a 100 percent perfect moment to take a risk. It is failure that comes from never taking action.

Thinking big is not just about understanding the potential or value of your product or services. It is also:

- **Understanding your own value**
- **Allowing yourself to dream with no limitations**
- **Creating a map that can possibly take you to the moon**

HOW WAS THE IMPOSSIBLE POSSIBLE?

THE ONLY REASON I was able to land an opportunity like this was because I knew my own potential. I believed in myself and was willing to think bigger than my limitations of no money or experience. By thinking big, you tap into a resource we all have called "creativity." Creativity sometimes requires risk. It involves uncertainty and will take you way out of your comfort zone. Creativity fuels growth for you and your business. Creativity is at the base of every big thinker.

YOUR TURN

THERE IS A SOLUTION to every problem in your business. How far are you willing to go and how hard are you willing to work to find it?

Name the three biggest challenges you're facing in your business today:

1.

2.

3.

Think about it: Why do you think you're facing them? Are they internal factors caused by you? Are there any external factors outside of your control present? What's the Number One reason you haven't made a shift in them?

FIVE
CONFIDENCE IS KEY

*"Regardless of where your company is right now—
good or bad—it's always your own fault."*

–Tiffany Largie

I was my first day as an official business owner. I was now the president of a well-known, well-established event planning and decorating company in Miami, Florida. My first day would be a special day indeed. I drove with the music loud and the windows down all the way to the shop, which was a good twenty-minute ride from my house. The sun seemed extra bright and beautiful…man, it was great. I was super excited.

As I pulled up to the shop, I noticed that something was missing. The sign! The stupid sign at the top of the building was nowhere to be found. Gone? I stared at the empty spot in complete disbelief. I couldn't park my car fast enough. As I approached the front door I noticed the door signs were gone too. Something was up. This was crazy.

Utterly confused, I walked inside to see the woman whom I bought the shop from in the far left corner. She appeared to be packing.

Why is she packing these? I thought to myself.

Don't get me wrong. I had imagined that she would be taking her personal items from the office, but this was different. The large items in her hands were not just picture frames, but marketing materials, fliers, postcards, stickers, brochures, and some business cards. Really, it was just about anything that had her name on it.

She turned to face me, smiled, and said, "Good morning." I wasn't smiling.

I walked closer to her and slowly asked where all of the signage had gone.

She looked at me and said calmly, "They are at my home."

I blurted out, "Your home; what are they doing there? I bought the business. I really need them!" Then I asked her to bring them back.

She paused for what seemed like an eternity.

Then she said to me, "Honey, you have everything you bought right here in this store."

She totally confused me with this one. Before I could ask her what she meant, she admitted to me that I didn't buy her business exactly; rather, I bought the company's assets. I gasped! Assets!

I did what? What the hell did that mean?

She looked at me squarely and said, "You get to keep the 'stuff' that's in the store." She told me her business name was her property, along with the phone number and website.

I was sick, so sick. Not a little sick. I was vomit-rush-me-to-the-flipping-hospital sick.

I stood there motionless. She could not be serious. I bought the flipping assets? What had I done? I just signed a note for $30,000 to pay for a business that I knew nothing about and surely had no money to invest in. I signed a lease for 12 months on top of that and now I stood in a building that had no signs, no phone lines, and no clear way to make money. I had been had.

LESSON: DON'T BUY A BUSINESS WITHOUT CONSULTING A LAWYER!

I KNOW THAT NOT all of us have the best perception of lawyers. If you have started your own business, it's very likely that you want to do everything yourself without anyone else's help, but trust me—sometimes it is far better to pay some money upfront and use the services of a professional. You will save yourself a lot of money and headaches in the long run.

Soon, she gathered her things and left the store. I cried for the first hour. I couldn't believe someone would do this. I was also afraid for anyone I knew to find out.

I needed a plan and I needed it quick. I sat in the store and waited for someone to walk in through the door, but hoping for a miracle wasn't going to work. I had to take some big steps for some big things to happen.

Again I had no experience, no money, and no customers. More importantly, I was the proud owner of a bunch of junk. I was wearing a hole in the carpet. After I stopped crying, I started pacing non-stop. I was terrified, actually horrified at what I had done. I had no idea how I was going to get customers to walk into that store.

I needed to come up with a plan quickly because I had just signed on the dotted line and committed myself to paying over $5,000 a month for the next six months! If this was not enough, I had my own bills to pay and now two kids to feed on my own. The pressure was on. My own expenses and paying for this business had lit a new fire under me that had never before existed. I found myself at a point where I was willing to do whatever it took.

I had a decision to make. I could continue to cry and kick myself, or I could realize I made a stupid mistake and needed to fix it. I had been down this road before. I had made stupid mistakes before. I knew that whatever it was, I had to fix it. So I turned once again to that principle…you have to be willing to do whatever it takes.

You have to be WILLING TO DO WHATEVER it takes.

In this case, I had to become an immediate event planner; selling a service is the fastest item that you can sell. Here, you are either selling knowledge or a skill. So I got on the phone and started asking people to allow me to plan their event. I didn't just ask people, I asked everyone. I started, like most people would, with my friends and family—they were the first ones I called. When I didn't get a bite, I decided it was time to get creative and find people whose customers would use my services. I called florists, photographers, videographers, bakers, musicians… I called everyone.

I was willing to make any deal to get a deal. Finally, just as I thought that I was going to exhaust every opportunity, a guy that I had spoken to earlier called me back. He had a couple in front of him who were in the midst of planning their wedding and interviewing wedding planners. I set up an appointment for the next day. The problem was that I didn't know anything about planning weddings. However, I knew where the library was and there was a Barnes & Noble not too far from it too. I was about to become an expert wedding planner. I read every wedding magazine and event planning book that I could get my hands on. I stayed up all night in order to become a wedding planning expert. Listen, if there was a way to become a wedding planning expert in 24 hours, I found it.

LESSON: PREPARATION GIVES YOU CONFIDENCE

APPROACHING THIS KIND OF opportunity with the limited knowledge I had about weddings would have been a poor decision. Whatever little knowledge I had was not current, so all of my reading preparation paid off in learning about food, locations, miserable guests, destination weddings, and trends. Confidence was the key here, not magic. It is not that I became confident after learning from the material I was reading. I became confident in myself. I am the greatest tool I have in all scenarios. And you, my dear, are the greatest tool that you have. After reading the hell out of all those magazines and books, I was ready to BUILD THE DAMN THING. All of it.

D-DAY

I GOT TO THE SHOP a little early the next morning, just to make certain that everything was perfect. At 10:00 sharp the couple walked in. I greeted them with big smiles and big hugs. I was ready. For two hours we sat together. Me, with my clipboard and notebook in hand, and them, holding each other's hand. They asked questions, and I had answers. They asked technical questions…and I had technical answers. They asked the what-if questions…I had some answers. Whatever answers I didn't have, I promised to deliver them within a week. I knew exactly what I wanted; I had a clear goal. I needed them to do two things before they left. First, I needed them to trust that I was the perfect match in helping them build the wedding of their dreams within their budget. Second, I needed them to leave a 25 percent deposit.

At the end of two hours, I wasn't out of answers, but they were surely out of questions. I went for it; I asked them for the partnership. I had no choice.

On my clipboard was an agreement for services that I had created the night before. I handed it to the bride. At first, the two were silent and then, for what seemed like forever, the bride spoke up and started a narrative about how she wanted to take more time and think about it, but I jumped in and mentioned that my calendar for the rest of that season was getting booked.

I told them that I knew I was the best solution for them, but was afraid of not having room left if they didn't get on my calendar soon.

She then turned to the groom and told him that my confidence made her more confident in the ability to create the wedding she envisioned within the budget of $15,000. If her husband-to-be was okay with it, she wanted to move forward and was excited to get started. It took everything in me to keep my composure to a minimum. I quickly grabbed a calculator to figure out the deposit amount. Whoa! I said to myself…it was a whopping $3,750—whoo-hoo!!!

They wrote me a check. Oh my gosh, I could not believe it…I did it!

YOUR TURN
LET'S LEARN A LITTLE about your business.

1. **On a scale of 1-10, how would you rate your own expertise?**

2. **Now pick someone in your field who you admire. How would you rate their expertise on a scale of 1-10?**

3. **Is there a gap? Yes or no.**

4. **If yes, why the gap? What's the number one reason?**

LET'S WORKSHOP TOGETHER

WHAT THINGS CAN YOU DO, learn, or experience in the next three months that would give you a MEGA boost in your knowledge and expertise?

Note: Hanging out at Barnes & Noble is NOT an option!

List them here:
1.
2.
3.
4.
5.

What's your "get them done date?" Hint: It should be 90 days from today's date.

SIX

BOSS MAPS NEED BOSS MOVES & BOSS MOVES REQUIRE BOSS MAPS

"You may not be where you want to be, because you have not declared where you want to be."

—Tiffany Largie

HAVE YOU EVER BEEN on a road trip stuck in the back seat and the driver is playing music that is getting on your nerves? They've loaded their iPod and you've heard "Roar" by Katy Perry like seven times now! Not only that, but you have to use the bathroom and they only stop when they feel like it and, if not that, then the driver gets food when *they* are really hungry as opposed to 45 minutes ago when you first mentioned it. You pass something on the interstate that looks interesting and want to get off and take a look around or simply take a break from the drive itself. However, the driver makes the final decision and drives right past that Exit 62 you were hoping to stop at.

With music, possibly we can compromise, but the direction that the car is moving in…that's a whole separate conversation. I mean, really. The driver has COMPLETE control of the direction the car goes in.

Thing is, most entrepreneurs are not in the driver's seat in their business. They may have believed they were, but the truth is that they just jumped in the car when it started. Because the car is moving, they *think* it's them in the driver's seat, but really they have no real idea where they're going, and when certain stops do happen, they're not sure how they got there.

If you're running a business, there is only one seat for you in that car, and that's the driver's seat. If you are sitting in any other seat other than the driver's seat in your business, then that's just stupid.

The driver is vital in getting to the destination. They see the big picture. They are instrumental in the plan and own the creative elements since ultimately they are in control of the steering wheel. It's really easy to figure out quickly if you're in the driver's seat in your business. These simple signs will tell you.

You know your margins on EVERY product or service.

Do you know your exact margins? Do you know how much profit is in EACH deal or sale of that item or service you offer? I mean, seriously, you gotta know this one. How much money are you making in each sale, transaction, or contract? Yes, you must know how much you sold it for, because you have attached a dollar sign to it, but was it profitable? If so, how much and what is your average? You should know your individual profit in each deal you make, along with your average, over the course of a period of time. This is a first and a must. It's like the gas of your business; you can't really go very far in business without profit. Go back and take a peek at your past few deals or sales, do some quick math, and remove ALL your costs involved including some basics for operation. Did you make any money?

You know exactly where you're going and so does EVERYONE on your team.

Do you have a destination for your business? No one starts a road trip and has no idea where they're going. Even though on that road trip you may not end up anywhere special or specific, you have to leave your home knowing in what direction you're going. You'll need to decide a few vital things like how much time you'll be gone for and in what direction you're headed. North, south, east, or west?

Do you have a destination? Where are you headed in your business? 50K, 500K, or 50 million? You will make stops such as 500K and 2.5 million along the way, but where are you actually headed in the end? How much time do you have to get there? Without a destination, you could possibly get on that highway and drive around in circles for hours or days wasting a whole lot of time, gas, and money…that would suck. If you don't have a clear destination, create one. Create a final destination and then work backwards like a true road trip, planning those stops along the way.

You know your numbers.

Off the top of your head, you should be able to answer these key questions about your business…I mean it *is* your business after all, right? How many customers did you sell to this week, month, and quarter? How does that compare to where you were last quarter or this time last year? What product or service in your business did you sell the most of this month? How many customers does it take to get to the destination? Did you reach that number this month? If not, how many customers, services, and products were you short? This is an important one and may take a little time, so take a day and dive deep into the questions posed here. Take these questions and workshop them. You'll find the answers—they're among your data. Once you have them, you'll be so far ahead in your business and ahead of most entrepreneurs in their business.

If you jump in your car and drive each day and never check to see how much gas you have at any given time, then you may find one day you start driving and your car leaves you stranded because it finally ran out of fuel. Likewise, if you don't know how much it's gonna take to fill up that tank and you're far from home with a five-dollar-bill in your hand, chances are you will run out of gas before you get to your destination…or any destination.

ANOTHER DRIVING SCENARIO

YOU START A ROAD TRIP with a destination in mind, but how do you know if you're getting close? You ask the driver and they say, "Trust me, I've driven from Nashville to New York many times." So you hope you're headed north, but how do you know for sure? Truth is, you don't. Without a map or GPS in hand, you are guessing—there is no accurate way to determine how close you are to your destination, what cities you'll pass along the way, how much longer you have until you get there, or where the gas stations will be.

It's getting dark and you look down at your watch. You realize you guys have been on the road for almost 15 hours! How is this even possible? Wasn't this drive supposed to take a little under 12 hours? You ask the driver where you are...but before you get the answer you see a sign that says, "Welcome to Illinois!"

You pull over and frantically search for a map in the glove compartment, but instead find a...GPS. You pull this thing out, baffled. Turning to the driver you say, "You mean to tell me that you had a GPS all this time and you didn't plug it in?!"

Radio silence.

Finally they respond, "Well, I thought I knew where we were going and didn't think that we needed it."

This trip sucks. We wasted time, we wasted money, and no one is interested in Chicago...we are nowhere near the end goal.

LESSON: MOVEMENT DOES NOT EQUAL PROGRESS

I BET IF I ASKED you which seat you were in in your business, by default you would say the driver's seat. This situation here is common in small businesses. We have an idea mentally of where we want to end up, but we did not have a map to get us there. We have a kick-off meeting, we come back from another amazing business conference, we finish reading that book or watching that highly-promoted webinar called, "Skyrocket your profits in 60 days!"

We started and are now moving in some direction…right? No, we're not. We're JUST moving. I call this the "busy effect." It's an illusion that makes you think that there is progress and somehow you find yourself "busy," but it's really because you have found meaningless ways to occupy your time with activities that don't produce revenue and cannot strongly tie back to a map or strong measurable growth.

What a bummer it is when we figure out that we are moving in the wrong direction. You usually find out months or years later when you are running out of cash or the genetic makeup of your business is almost identical to when you started. You didn't grow, and if you did grow, it wasn't in the direction that you needed to go.

These three things are everything: **time, energy and money**. We only have three options at this point…

SOLUTION 1: Stop, rest, and refuel.

We find a place to stay overnight to recharge and refuel with a plan to get back on the road hopefully the next day.

Problem: Now we are trying to get ourselves ready overnight for a brand new trip. We waste resources, lose money, and waste time.

SOLUTION 2: Make an immediate U-Turn.

Yes, we can backtrack to where we started and try the route again.

Problem: We are very tired, have little energy left, and no room for thinking.

Stress levels have risen and overall it's not a good environment for growth. We lost good resources, lost money, and wasted precious time.

SOLUTION 3: Let's stay here.

We were tired so we got some rest, refueled, and we decided to see what Chicago had to offer. We were already there, after all, and the truth is we were tired!

Problem: For a while it may seem okay and acceptable, just like in your small business, but Chicago is not the right place for you. Your business is now in a space that doesn't have the right elements that you need to push and sustain growth. By staying in Chicago, you've not only wasted resources, money, and time, but when you realize the kind of growth you need is not possible, you end up heading to New York anyway.

Do you see the point I am trying to make? Had we plugged in the stupid GPS before we left, we would have sailed to New York, gotten there in record time. We would have used the magic of the GPS to avoid traffic, detours, and accidents. Spending a few minutes programming the GPS would have made all the difference on the journey.

Now, let me take this a step further. Had we taken an hour at some point to do a little planning and mapping out for food, gas, and some sightseeing we would have been WAY ahead of the game. In business, we have complete control over whether or not we want to, or choose to, plug in the GPS. I don't care how big you are. Every business needs to have the GPS on every day, all day. When you get to your destination, you spend a little time there and then you set a new course. This is how you grow.

You are not just plugging the GPS in for yourself as the owner, you are plugging it in for your team as well. Your team needs to know where you're headed, so they can know where they're headed. If you jump into something and have no clear idea where you're headed, it could be a little scary in general. You don't want to send that vibe to your team, or to your customers. Clarity on where you're going creates an open environment where everyone is more engaged and moves more confidently in their individual roles as they move toward the common goal. Don't be a victim of the "I think I know how to get there" or the "Where the hell are we going" syndromes.

For this reason alone we must build a map.

You need a BBG…a "Build-it Big Guide!" We are calling it a Business Dream Map. This activity will help you quickly and easily figure out if the plan you are working on now will get you where you want. Go ahead, stop reading and grab it now at **www.dtdtnation.com/buildthedamnthing**. Trust me, you will be glad you did.

After visiting my website, I would be curious to see how close and quickly your current map will get you to the life you are after. Please let me know: send me an email **tiffany@tiffanylargie.com** OR find me on social media **@tiffanylargie** and let me know!

From a map in general I can quickly identify the following: what direction I am going, north, south, east or west, I can see a couple of the major cities that I will pass along the way, if there are elevation paths of difference, and which areas have a little more congestion due to population and roads.

So let's figure out where your starting point is, and then figure out exactly where you are and where you want to be.

What I love about the GPS is that I can plug it in no matter where I am and instantly get a clear map and path to get me where I need to be. No matter where you are in your business, you build a map to grow your business. Nonetheless, when you're not starting from home, it could be a little overwhelming. So, the natural question is, where do I start? What's the best area for me to start thinking bigger?

YOUR TURN

Why did you start this business?

What was the goal?

Are we there yet?

What will it take to close the Gap? Be specific.

Though it's important to be clear on where we are going before we work on remapping, it's a good idea to get some clarity on why we started the journey in the first place.

As I mentioned above, I have created a short planning guide completely free for you so that you can map out what you want your business to look like, and what it will take to get there.

SEVEN
THE MONEY IS ALWAYS IN THE DETAILS

"You don't need it to be good; you need it to be great."

–Tiffany Largie

W AY BACK IN THE flip-phone days, I had a super cool, blue flip-phone made by Motorola. I paid my bill every month and I even paid extra for the insurance Sprint offered at the time. I thought I was set. One day, that changed.

I woke up on a Tuesday morning ready to board a plane to Washington, D.C. and all of sudden, my phone screen went black. You've been there before or you know someone who has been in this situation. You charge the phone for hours and the stupid thing still won't turn on.

This was my first time.

I had no idea what to do, though after my five-minute panic attack, I happily remembered something. I had paid for insurance on my monthly phone bill for the last two years faithfully and was safe. Naturally, I called Sprint customer service and explained my problem to them. The woman on the other line was pleasant, telling me she was sorry to hear about my problem and that she could help. I was relieved. Help was on the way. My problem was going to be solved and the day was saved. So she went through what seemed like a fairly long process of collecting information and placing me on hold. Finally, she informed me she was sending me a label and that when I got it, I needed to ship the phone back to them, and after 30 days or so they would determine whether or not I had a problem.

I was royally pissed.

Here I am standing in the airport with my broken phone and she was telling me that I needed to send the phone in to determine whether or not I had a problem! Not her, but the company, was positioning her to make me feel like a liar. I am looking at the phone in my hand, the screen is black… I have a problem. I surely did not feel like a valued customer. I had spent my hard-earned dollars with this relationship for quite some time. I expected to have better treatment after the initial sale. As if that wasn't enough, she was also trying to tell me that I would be out of a phone for up to 30 days.

Angry, I asked her the most important question of that day. "What am I supposed to do for 30 days without a phone?"

She paused and said, "Motorola, nor Sprint, provide a program, or rather an answer, to that question. We don't provide temporary phones." She paused again, "Maybe you can borrow a phone from someone to use in the interim?"

Maybe. Are you flipping kidding me? You're telling me to figure it out? How can I be the customer who has paid all this money for insurance and you are giving me half of a solution!

She was quiet. I was heated.

She asked me if I wanted her to send me the label or not. This for me was an absolute Epic Fail for Sprint and the manufacturer.

I told her no, thanked her for her time, and then I hung up the phone and stared down at this stupid blank phone. I realized this was not her own doing because this customer service rep does not own Sprint nor Motorola, nor could she get me to directly access Motorola so I could talk to them about their product!

She was simply carrying out her orders with whatever plan was laid out in front of her.

I had a serious problem and no answer. I didn't know what to do.

Somehow I began to remember a commercial I had seen in the last week about a phone provider focused on customer service…it was AT&T introducing the new BlackBerry 8830. In the professional space at that time, everyone I knew had a BlackBerry, so I figured this was the best place for me to go. With hours until my flight left, I headed to the nearest AT&T store, which was about twenty minutes away.

I walked inside, and before I could look around, a nice guy quickly walked over to me with a big smile on his face and said, "You look like you're in a hurry. How can I help you quickly?" We both chuckled a bit and I explained to him my dilemma. I informed him that I was here specifically to pick up the new BlackBerry 8830.

"Why?" he asked. I told him I had heard that BlackBerry was a reliable product and company and that it would give me the basic work functions that I needed. To be honest, anything at that time would have been an upgrade from my Motorola flip-phone that by then I had had for about two years.

Even though he knew I was in a rush, he didn't seem eager in showing me the BlackBerry section that was directly in front of us. Instead, he asked me a little bit about what I did for a living and how I would be using my phone. I was taken aback by this. When buying my phone at the Sprint store, I had never been asked any questions about how I would use the phone. I told him I'd use it to make calls for work, retrieve voicemails, and hopefully now answer emails like I had seen on the commercials. I then added that I got quite a bit of phone calls and that my phone was being used all the time. He wanted to know how I retrieved my voicemails from my current phone, and as I explained it to him, he confirmed that it was the antiquated way of communication on a whole. I was behind the times. Do you remember when we used to dial in and then wait for the audio of each voicemail to play? You'd have to wait for each voicemail to play and then press prompts to replay or skip to the next one.

I told him that I did this and I hated the process. He then asked if he could take just a second more of my time to show me another phone that's not made by BlackBerry. I was hesitant, but he was already moving toward my right, so I followed. A moment later, there we stood in front of the iPhone display. It was a huge display. Before he could show me anything more I quickly spoke up.

I said, "I don't want a fancy phone or anything. I won't be using my phone to play games or anything like that. Just work."

He smiled and said, "I have something to show you." But instead of reaching for the phone on the display counter in front of us, he reached into his own pocket and pulled out his own personal iPhone. I was intrigued.

He didn't explain what he was doing, but he moved around that screen and quickly pulled up his voicemails and there was a list. He showed me how easy it was for him to stop certain voicemails midstream, replay, skip, and play only the ones that I recognized because the iPhone listed the voicemails! I could see all my voicemails at once in a list format and could choose which one to listen to and when! I was impressed.

He showed me nothing else about the phone, but then proceeded to tackle my other concerns: durability and support. "I'm able to go to any nearby Apple store at the mall or down the street and get instant support from them, the manufacturer, 'anytime,'" he told me. They were always able to address his problems right there and then. No wait, no hassle, and more importantly...no drama. As he was telling me about his experience, I saw we were now moving toward the front door of the store itself to look at the parking lot. I had no idea why we were going there.

He then explained to me that one of the things that made the iPhone incomparable in the market at the time was its durability and the fact that Apple made cases for their phones, which helped with wear and tear.

I laughed and said, "That case doesn't look very strong."

He laughed back and declared, "The Otter Box has no comparison." Before I could blink, he threw his phone out the front door and into the parking lot!

My jaw dropped.

"What do you think you're doing?" I started yelling.

He simply stated, "I needed to show you just how serious Apple is about making sure your device has extra protection. They collaborated with a company that makes this thing almost indestructible." He walked out and grabbed the phone off the pavement in an empty parking space to hand it to me. The phone was unharmed.

My mouth was still wide open, I was speechless. He was smiling. Not only was my experience second to none...he had also made the moment memorable.

I bought the iPhone and instantly became a fan.

It wasn't but six weeks later I was traveling to catch another plane. I felt like it was déjà vu. The phone was blank, completely dark, and it simply wouldn't turn on. Ugh. I couldn't look up the closest Apple store fast enough, which was thirty minutes away. I got dressed, ran out the door, and drove like a mad woman to this location. I had never been to an Apple store; what an impressive first impression.

Right out of the gate, someone greeted me at the door and looked eager and ready to help me. Man, I was almost excited. This girl asked how she could help me and I quickly explained that my phone was blank and I had just bought it at a local AT&T store, but couldn't find the receipt.

She said, "No problem," grabbed a device, and then added me to a list. She told me it would be about a fifteen-minute wait.

When my name was called fifteen minutes later, I was beyond anxious. I handed the guy my phone with no box and no receipt. He asked for my name and then went to open the phone. Honestly, I couldn't tell what he was doing over the counter. For the purpose of this, we will call it trouble-shooting. After about two minutes or so, he placed the phone to the side, turned around and went under the counter and took out another box. He returned and began to explain that he was not sure why my phone wasn't working, but since I was under a one year warranty, he was just going to replace it right there and then.

If you're wondering if I was speechless again, then you're right. I almost had to clean up the drool—it was crazy. A few minutes later, I had a new phone in my hands, fully connected and working.

He looked at me and said, "I am so sorry you had this experience and that you had to be without a phone for this morning. Hopefully this didn't put you too far back in your day. If you have any more problems with your phone, please just come back in and let us know. We are more than happy to help."

No joke…I had just fallen in love.

Apple had just made me what I call a "raving fan."

The funniest part about my new relationship is that my phone bill was twenty-five percent more than what I was paying with Sprint and fourteen percent higher than what I would have paid for with the BlackBerry.

Here is the cherry on top. Forty-eight hours later I got an email asking me about my experience at the Apple store, which they call the Genius Bar. A week later, that sales rep called me back to find out how I liked my new iPhone and to see if I had any questions or needed anything else.

RAVING FANS…NOT OPTIONAL

I HAVE TO TELL YOU that this is a big deal for me. It's free, it's easy, and it's a must for any business striving beyond just being a good company with good customers.

This is where we reach pure awesomeness in our business. It's having customers who are so flipping in love with you that they randomly start talking about your company to a non-user as if they had stock in the doggone place.

When you can take the customer through such an amazing experience, that not only leaves them in awe, but more importantly, leaves them wanting more, you create what I call a "raving fan."

Now, just so that you and I are clear. Your customers are not only the people who buy your product or interact with your brand. Your customers are also the people who come to work every day at your company. To be honest with you, employees are actually your first customers.

There are two different types of customers that every business must be committed to serving: your internal customer, and your external customer.

Both customers add to your bottom line and both customers will propel your business in a way that no other form of strategy can. When they market for you by talking about your product, they talk from a unique place that no brochure, website, business card, fl, or mailer could ever do. They talk from their experience. Experience is unique in marketing because people believe other people. It's just that simple. I mean think about it. When I visit a city, one of the first things I do when I check in is ask the front desk what's the best thing to eat around here.

Now I have done my research on nearby restaurants before I walked in, but there is nothing like hearing from someone else what their personal experience was like. I could have decided before I got there on my own, picked the top three choices, and then asked what they thought of them. One of two things would happen. They would give me a big smile and a silent thumbs up and tell me not only is the place great, actually one of their favorites, or would quickly tell me that they would not recommend me going…and then direct me in another direction. I don't know about you, but for me, nine out of ten times I am going to listen to that person's experience.

If we reached out to one of your customers that spent money with your company in the last 90 days and we asked them about their experience with your company and your brand, what would they say?

Are you certain of the answer?

If the response is bad, though I know sometimes its subjective, BUT I would also say…that Houston we have a WHOLE problem.

If the response is "good," in my book, there is a HUGE opportunity! There was something missing, we can ask them what—and get to GREAT!

Let me tell you what a "good" really does to your bottom line.

Good will not give you a strong referral base. Good will not help you bring repeat customers. Good will not create a raving fan.

Good will not grow your business quickly.

What "good" really does is give your competitors a clear road and an avenue to amplify your weaknesses so that they can create an experience for your customer that's pure awesomeness.

By now you're wondering how one can go from good to great, or rather… from great to awesomeness. Most companies focus on making sure that the sales interaction is great. You've seen it. You go to your favorite restaurant and they recite key phrases when taking your order, like "My pleasure," "Come again soon," and "We look forward to seeing you again."

Yes, these sayings are a good way to shape the customer experience during the time of sale, but the secret that is often overlooked here is that the customer experience starts way before they actually purchase and should not end when you give them a receipt. Most of us are so focused on the middle, leaving little focus on the beginning or end.

I call this "The Total Customer Experience."

You can do huge things here in your business today just by thinking through when that first interaction actually really starts and when it ends…let's map this together.

Stop for a moment and answer these questions:

1. **What is the first place the customer interacts with my company?**
2. **What unique phrases do we say in the midst of the actual transaction?**
3. **How do we ensure absolute satisfaction after they have bought the product?**

4. **What about ways after they bought the product?**
5. **In what ways do we encourage them to interact with us again until possibly the next purchase?**

If any of these are blank for you, it's because you're missing something and currently giving your customer a "good" experience.

But you don't need good; you need it to be great. You need raving fans.

EIGHT
MEDIOCRE APPLICATION FOR A MEDIOCRE RETURN

"It's better to have no representation,
than bad representation."

–TIFFANY LARGIE

Now onto BEING more; this is a WHOLE subject in itself. Let's go. Listen, small business owner, it doesn't matter if you are just one person, ten people, or a team of a hundred. You absolutely must be 100 percent at your game at all times. Mediocrity and boss moves have been archenemies for a very long time. You may not have a lot of money, but you do have resources, and you can be creative. Regardless of your size, you must act big in every move you make, especially those moves that give you direct contact either to your customer, or more importantly, a prospective customer.

YOU DON'T HAVE TO BE A FAKE

BEING BIG IS NOT about faking it until you make it. You either are or you aren't in your own mind. Being big in this sense really starts with your state of mind and some decisions. It's about putting your best foot forward and giving your prospective customer or client a name or storefront that makes them feel unbelievably confident to do business with you.

Ten to fifteen years ago, it was hard to present yourself as anything bigger than what you were without flat-out lying. Times have really changed.

With little money, any business can effectively and inexpensively present a strong front allowing them to compete with the biggest in their market with confidence. I just love that. The tools available today really allow for the best talent and capabilities to be shown in the market even if you are tiny.

All small business owners, listen clearly and carefully: there are no excuses for mediocrity. Absolutely none.

Let's look at three key areas of any business that will immediately damage your credibility and force you to hand your competitor your sale because of mediocrity.

HOW DO YOU SHOW UP IN PERSON?

SOMETIMES YOU HAVE TO judge books by their cover. You just have to. There have been plenty of times that I have walked through Barnes & Noble and picked up a book just because the cover looks so doggone good. We humans judge everything and everyone all day long based on the presentation. This is true for food, neighborhoods, stores, and especially true for people. Hence, I don't believe in that saying "Don't judge a book by its cover." I feel like if it's a good book, then it should have an even greater cover. It's just that simple.

Let me start by saying these two things. Being an entrepreneur and owning a small business is a 24/7 gig. No matter what you think, people are judging your look. It's how you present your business, period. You need to be concerned all day, every day, about how you've shown up in the world to whoever is looking. The reality is that we are all working in customer sales and service now, even if that isn't part of our formal job description.

Yes, you may have clients that you serve primarily from 9-5, Monday through Friday, so who cares what you look like on Friday night going to the movies? Or Saturday morning running to the grocery store? No one will see you in either space, right? In one outing, you'll be in the dark for two hours and the other it's in and out, 10 minutes max. The idea is that no one will see you anyways, right? Wrong! You are your business and your business is you. You must be prepared at all times to sell something to someone, or make the much-needed connection with the person you struck up a conversation with while behind that couponer in the grocery aisle. You are never off-duty. Never. I am not saying that when you are out you're scoping the crowd for someone to deliver a thirty-second pitch to every seven minutes. You have to be prepared for an opportunity, and you never know where it's coming from. Money is money, right? Who cares what time of day you make it?

Don't just put on anything to go out of the house. Seriously, how many times do I run into someone at the grocery store and strike up a conversation? You're standing there talking and you build rapport and somehow the conversation turns into what do you do for a living. That person has already looked you over from head to toe, up and down. Do you look credible or do you look homeless? Do you look like someone they can trust with a service or their money? It's simple: when you're leaving your house, stop by a mirror and ask, "Is what I'm wearing something I would be happy to give an impromptu talk in to my target audience, or no?" Are the clothes you're wearing a good representation of your brand or business? Do they lend you credibility? Do they *really* represent you? If the answer is no, then please just take them off.

LESSON: DON'T LEAVE THE HOUSE IF YOU WOULD BE EMBARRASSED TO BE SEEN BY YOUR BEST CUSTOMER

NOTHING FRUSTRATES ME MORE than calling a business and hearing a weak, unexcited hello on the other end. Ugh, I hate that. I really do. My first gut reaction is to hang up. It's like, if you're not excited about my call, I'm not excited about your company. It's a two-way street. Most of the time, I'll say back to that miserable person, "Gee, is the product/service that bad over there? Never mind; I'll be calling your competitor. I am sure they will be HAPPY I called."

If it's not that, it's the person who takes all of their calls on their cell phone and makes it obvious. I think I'm calling a big company only to have someone pick up the phone with a baby crying in the background. What? I thought I called a company, not someone warming up bottles. Both just fail, no matter how much you slice it.

When someone calls you, you've got less than five seconds to make a great first impression on them. Please, please, please make it good. Like, really good. Actually, make it awesome!

There are two key ingredients in creating a dynamic intro for your company over the phone: consistency and excitement. For this recipe you MUST have both!

Keep these three rules in mind when building consistency with your phone strategy:

1. **Create a happy script. You must nail every call no matter what. You just never know who is on the other end and what impact they are going to have on your bottom line. Write a script that forces the same introduction to the call every time no matter what.**

2. **Consider an automated greeting. There are so many tools out there that can help you put your very best foot forward with little set up. Take, for example, an online phone service like Google Voice or RingCentral. It's great for $20 bucks a month you . It's great. For ten bucks a month you have a phone number that your customer calls and hears a greeting, giving you enough time to get yourself together and answer the phone. You can dial or receive calls through the Internet and add an app to your smartphone. One big plus here is that these services will give depth to your company. You can create extensions directing them to mention other departments in your company even if they all lead right back to you. So on your caller ID you'll see that it's**

a transferred call from the service giving you a little time to prepare, and if you choose to answer you can put down the baby, move away from the chicken frying, or better yet…get out of the bathroom and take the call. Get creative; put your best foot forward.

3. Consider a phone service or virtual assistant. They are pleasant, stationary and can handle any script or guide you give them. Again, this is a low-cost option averaging $100-300 a month. Now you have a live person answering your calls, again creating depth in your company, and more importantly, creating some consistency. You don't have to take the call yourself, and you also don't miss the call either. They will know what to say and how to say it, and with the right virtual assistant or answering service, they can possibly begin to help you mold and shape your brand and customer perception.

YUP, YOUR VIRTUAL FRONT TOO!

BE HONEST; DOES YOUR online presence clearly say, "Yes, dammit, I am open, fresh, current, and ready for interaction?" Or does your online presence say, "Hmmmm…catch me if you can?"

Your customer moves from your Facebook page to your Twitter page and then to your actual site—what do they see? How does your presence compare to five others in your market? Does your online presence tell your story successfully for you? The customer may not know what story you're telling if there isn't a lot of activity and the ability to engage with you and your community is low. The same amount of interaction you need in person, at networking events, and at conferences, is the same level of activity and effectiveness that you ultimately need online on a consistent basis. This is the exact same way that you need to treat social media and your web presence. Take a peek at the different places you show up online right now. If you have something up that's representing your company, but you know in your heart is not your best foot forward…then get rid of it! It is better to have no representation than to have bad representation.

Then there is that same question again: "How do you show up?" Would you want your best customer to see that post on Facebook? Or that comment on Twitter? Don't put anything out there that you don't want your best customer to see. Again, when you own a business, you are working twenty-four hours a day, seven days a week. All things in social media are fair game when considering whether or not to do business with you.

As far as I am concerned, marketing and branding your business online is not optional. Most of it is free, but you can pay for what you can't do yourself by outsourcing to cheap online sources like Fiverr. There is really no excuse.

INSTANT SUCCESS...NO WAIT NEEDED

BACK IN 2013, I BELIEVE I witnessed one of the most creative business moves I have seen in a long time; it proved the importance and power of social media. We are all used to the traditional way of putting out an album by a musical artist. There is a huge focus right before the release on different forms of media like print ads, TV, and radio. Beyoncé, however, made a decision to skip this process all together and instead focused her efforts to release her album inexpensively (virtually free) on social media.

Of all the social media platforms one could use to communicate something about music, she chose Instagram. I couldn't believe it, personally. Not only did she release it at midnight in the middle of December when the focus should be on the holidays, but she released the whole album, 14 songs along with 17 videos available on iTunes, and sold 828,773 copies in just three days! This was mega power—she superseded her previous albums' downloads and the product was a success! The point is that she used social media as the only platform to sell her product. Let me tell you, this movement is here to stay. Your customers are on one social media platform or another. I promise you. Don't believe me? Let's look at the stats.

There are many different social media platforms these days that you may hear circulating around. There is Facebook, Twitter, Instagram, YouTube,

Tiktok, Vimeo, Pinterest, LinkedIn, Meetup, and the list continues. I am going to narrow the focus, and we are going to take a peek at the most prominent for your own business.

STATS

LET'S START HERE: Seventy-two percent of all Internet users are on Facebook! Seventy-two percent. To put this into perspective, there are over three billion people on the Internet right now in the world, which means this social media platform gives you access to over 2.1 billion people at once! That, my friend…is huge.

FACEBOOK is where the party is. Make no mistake about it.
- 2.93 BILLION active MONTHLY users
- 1.96 BILLION active DAILY users
- 67 percent of active users check the site daily
- 51 percent of users check it multiple times a day
- 63 percent of marketers report that Facebook is critical or important to their business
- Said to be the most popular worldwide

TWITTER
- Has more than 396 million registered users
- Has 217 MILLION active DAILY users
- 46 percent of all adults online tweet on a regular basis
- 85 percent of followers feel more connected with a small business after following them on Twitter
- 42 percent of Twitter users use Twitter to learn about products and services
- 75 percent of small businesses are on Twitter

LINKEDIN
- 830 MILLION active MONTHLY users
- 59 percent of online adults are on LinkedIn

- 40 percent of them check it daily
- 41 percent of millionaires use LinkedIn
- 59 percent of LinkedIn users don't visit Twitter

The platform that fascinates me the most right now is TikTok. Let's just take a look at these stats. The whole platform is based on REELS. Short, 90-second and under videos that deliver an entire concept from beginning to end. This is my definition.

TIK TOK

- **TikTok has over 1 billion monthly active users. This is MORE than Twitter and more than Linkedin even though it's one of the newest to the social media game.**
- **47 percent of TikTok users are between ages 10-29**
- **Nearly 80+ million monthly active users are in the United States**
- **37 percent of TikTok users have a household income of $100k+**
- **60 percent of all TikTok users are female.**
- **53 percent of TikTok creators are between 18 and 24.**

There has NEVER been an easier time for you to put your brand, product or service, and yourself in front of your target audience. Look, it's pretty clear. Your customers, wherever they are, are definitely on one social media platform or the other. You have to get there too. This is another must for your business. It doesn't have to be perfect; you just need to start. Start somewhere. Looking at the stats alone, I would personally start with Facebook. It clearly is the place to be at this point for any-sized business, regardless of what product or service you're dishing up. Once you're on Facebook, you need to make sure you're doing **two things:**

1. **Make sure that you know where your customers are hanging out. Groups, interests, associations, or affiliations through shared "Likes." Look for them, get close, make friends, and build relationships. Those relationships will turn into trust and trust in business turns into money.**

2. After you are clear on where they are hanging out, give them a reason to want to hang out with you. It's like your house when guests are coming over. You want to make sure that everything is tidy and neat and the place looks inviting. You don't want them to come over and instantly think of running in the other direction. You know how to clean up your house for guests. Get to work!

Your business should be gathering your people into one of all of the below **DAILY**:

- **Email List**
- **Text Message List**
- **Phone Call List**
- **Private social groups like groups on Facebook, or groups on Linkedin.**
- **Your local community—invite them to your office often.**

Gathering people, nurturing them, and re-educating them on a regular basis as to why you are the best is a must. It's the foundation of how you keep your business pipeline consistent and full. I have a list of tools for you to take a peek at that we use for all of our companies. Head to **www.dtdtnation.com/buildthedamnthing** to get access to the list at no cost.

The same question applies here: "How do you show up?" This applies to being a business owner and your company as well. You should have both a personal profile and a business profile. You need to maximize the different platforms and options on both, as well as increase your customer capacity. A business page really allows you to establish a brand that is true to your business. Here is what visitors are looking for when they pull up your business page:

- **Is the information current?**
- **Is the information relevant?**

- **Is it a bunch of stuffy information or is this company authentic and real?**
- **Can I touch the people inside? Are they like me?**
- **Is this company likable?**
- **Is the page consistent?**
- **Does the page look good?**
- **Are they engaged with their customers by being responsive?**
- **Is it a two-way street? Or are they just putting out information?**

This is not a book about social media…BUT social media is a **big** part of how you BUILD THE DAMN THING. In order to do it right. You gotta show up, and show up strong…showing up is not optional. Give it some time, plant a social media seed now, and watch it grow. It will take awhile, and yes, you must water it every day…but eventually it will grow and bloom dollars.

Don't skip out on the next set of questions. You don't want to miss this opportunity to build your business. Don't skip this section. Whip out your pen, prepare to write below, and let's get to work!

QUICK SOCIAL MEDIA CHECK

1. **Do you have a Facebook business page so that you can run ads?**

2. **How often are you posting to your social media platforms?**

3. When was the last time you made an update to your website?

4. When was the last social media post that you put up?

5. Are your posts related to your brand, product, or service?

6. Are you getting likes? If so, how many?

7. When was the last time you wrote a blog on LinkedIn or your website?

8. Do you have a place where the market can dive into you—just the CEO—as a brand, in addition to your product and or service?

Now stop. Get out a sheet of paper and write down the names of your top five competitors. Answer these same eight questions about them. Although this may take a little while, it is well worth the time. You'll discover something huge through it. I promise.

Continue writing with me below. Now let's map this thing out, and get some answers!

9. What is my brand? (You should be able to articulate this.)

10. Who are my customers?

11. Where are they hanging out online?

12. **Who are my top five competitors that are using social media that I admire?**

13. **Which platform do they use the most OR have the most followers? (Hint: You should be there too!)**

14. **What type of things are they posting? Pictures? Articles? How-tos?**

15. **Do you have any of them?**

You have answered these questions. Now what? Let's go one step further to clean up your storefront. Below is your first step. Complete this and you are well on your way to dominating and growing your business.

What are your social media handles? We have one for each company, and I have a separate one for me, the CEO. I'll use mine as an example:

- Facebook.com/TiffanyLargie
- Twitter.com/TiffanyLargie
- Pinterest.com/TiffanyLargie
- Instagram.com/TiffanyLargie
- TikTok.com/Tiffanylargie

Note: everything after the "/" is called your "handle," and one can assume that after heading to the desired platform when they type in the "@" and then your name like this, they should find you. Such as typing in **@tiffanylargie** on any social media platform you chose. You'll find me. I mirror that same handle to have a conversation with my followers or customers anywhere in the world, keeping everything consistent with **@tiffanylargie**. It helps visitors find me quickly. Do you have a different name for each social media platform? If so, let's fix that! Go ahead and do that RIGHT NOW; make all of your social media handles the same.

The important thing is to just get started. Social media is not going anywhere. Many older business owners may tend to not see the value in these platforms—these sites might just seem like diversions. Don't make the same mistake. They can actually unlock enormous revenue potential.

NINE
EATING TOLERATIONS FOR LUNCH AND DINNER? JUST STOP.

"Your very first, most bestest customers
are always going to be your employees."

–Tiffany Largie

Mediocrity has absolutely no place in your business. None. Mediocrity is only for small thinkers. If you have gotten this far, I know you are on your way to bigger thinking in your business, so I will proudly say that small thinking is simply not for us anymore and with this we will be getting rid of mediocrity in our business forever. You need to put your foot down and vow that you will accept only the best—both from those you work with and from yourself.

Now, let's start with vendors. Vendors can't provide mediocre service or products and you simply can't accept them either. That's right. We will not be accepting any work provided for us that is just okay. There is a tendency from time to time within small businesses to accept mediocrity. They do it because they just don't know better. There are three common ways that small businesses accept and suffer from these habitual mediocrity offenders if they don't put their foot down.

I AM TOO SMALL
Some will accept mediocrity from a large company because they feel

too small and insignificant in comparison to that larger entity. Your money is green and it is just as good as any other customer that they have been spending money with. You deserve the exact same attention, respect, and dedication as anyone else who's spending money. If you're not getting that, then it's time to find new vendors. It's vital that you speak up and demand to get the same treatment, respect and quality of work in response to the tangibles and intangibles that any other company does. The last thing anyone wants, no matter the size, is a bad review from a customer who says that they didn't meet their expectations. You must hold them to a higher expectation, the same expectation that your customers hold you to. Aren't your customers quick to tell you when something is missed? Or when you were late, or simply didn't get it right? Now, I don't believe that small businesses accept mediocrity on purpose, but I think they accept it by not really being clear on the value of their own business. Whether you're one person, ten people, or a hundred people, you've got vendors and you've got to hold those vendors to the exact same standards you provide to your customers—anything below that is simply unacceptable. As an entrepreneur, you work too damn hard for your money. You really do. Every dollar came with a fight. You had to earn it, so why would you spend that hard-earned money with someone who doesn't value it like you do?

A FRIEND HELPED ME

SOME ACCEPT IT BECAUSE they failed to do their homework and weren't aware that a better option existed. The rest accept it because they are letting a "friend" help them. We rely on friends to help us out because financially they will give you a break whether they discount the service or do it at no cost.

I am going to spend some time here, because this one is really important to me. Personally, I am not a fan of using a friend or family to provide me a service for free. In my experience when someone is doing something for free, unless it's my core family, they are not doing it one hundred percent. They are not using the best resources or materials to accomplish the task.

I find that they rush and cut either corners or time. I expected the website to be up and running in two weeks and now we are on week six! Hey, it was free; we should be grateful because we got something for nothing, right? Wrong. Your business is not a hobby.

You're here to make money, grow, and solve problems. You can't do those things if you have parts of your business depending on others that you're not paying. Vendors have to be committed to delivering the service on time; they need to be incentivized. This is where something of value comes in to secure the commitment, which is money. It's better to not have it than to have something that does not represent your brand, or help you meet your objectives, or being in a sea of your own missed deadlines as they are constantly telling you that it will be done "next week" or "soon." You were better off without the free or discounted service.

EQUAL EXCHANGE

I FIND THE ONLY TIME it makes sense to allow friends or family members to do something for me is when I do something in return for them of value. Some call this act "bartering;" I call it an "equal exchange of quality services."

This equal exchange sets the tone for both sides to provide the same attention to details and quality as they would for a paying customer, because they are getting something of equal value in return. I have found this method over the years to be highly effective in times when I was just starting in business or didn't have enough cash flow. At times, it was for something small like new, quality business cards. Other times it has been for items in the thousands, or tens of thousands, like web design, video, photography, or office equipment.

I just want you to know that bartering *can* also be used to grow your current business in new areas with partnerships when you don't know the person and there is no relationship to stand on. You approach that person, identify what you want, and identify their need and how you can fill it. Then if they are open, you negotiate terms.

If you are crystal clear on the value of your business, then you won't accept anything that it doesn't deserve.

Money in entrepreneurship is not hard to come by, but you sacrifice a whole lot and go take on a whole lot to earn it. You work way too hard for every bit of revenue and profit your company brings in to squander it on something that's mediocre.

YOUR CUSTOMER DOESN'T ALWAYS KNOW BEST

I REMEMBER A FEW years ago I had a sales rep who had stopped in to check on a customer's account since he happened to be in the neighborhood that Friday, which was common. The client had a mid-sized company, but unfortunately, it was almost fifty minutes from our main office, so stopping in was a treat. We liked stopping in from time to time just to say hello and to see if we could be of any help. When he stopped in, he learned that our key contact in the IT department was no longer with the company and left his card for the new guy in charge. When he got back to the office later that day, he sent the gentleman in charge a follow-up email that went like this:

Hi XXXX,

I stopped in today just to say hello. I know you are busy, but let us know if you need anything, or if there is anything that we can do to help you.

Have a great weekend, XXXXX

For me this was a nice gesture on the sales rep's behalf. Within the hour, the rep got a response back. Shocked, he forwarded it to me with the words, "What did I do wrong?"

The note read:

XXXX,

If I wanted you to stop by I would have asked. I don't think I did. Furthermore, when we are ready to renew our contract in a few years, we will be going out to get other quotes.

XXXXX

I stared at the screen dumbfounded. Yes, I wanted the revenue from the customer, but I would tolerate that type of mediocrity from one manager to another. That was simply unacceptable. No money is worth anyone on my team putting up with such disrespect and rudeness.

I decided to reply myself to the customer and copied the rep on it:

XXXXX,

I am disappointed that you made a choice to respond to XXXXX in such a poor manner. He is one of our highest-rated account managers and all customers think highly of him because of his key attention to details and passion he has for our customers. From one manager to the next, that response you gave to him was unacceptable. The man was just doing his job and fulfilling his commitment to his customers. How many of your other vendors stop in just to "check in" knowing they can't get anything in return. If you are not interested in a committed partner providing you superior customer service, then please let me know personally so that I can make room in XXXXX's portfolio for a customer who is!

Thank you,

Tiffany Largie

I was totally prepared to let that customer go with no exceptions!

Funny enough…later that year the rep upgraded all of the customers' equipment. They didn't even look at other options. You cannot be afraid to let go of a customer or reprimand them. If you are indeed providing a quality service and/or product, they must hold up their end of the bargain as well. Trust me, those one or two customers that are bogging you down, complaining without valid reasons, and moreover, creating unneeded stress for you and your team, is not worth the money. No amount of money. The adage that "the customer is always right" only goes so far. When a customer's demands are an affront to your time and dignity, it is most certainly an appropriate opportunity to push back or part ways. Your time is simply too valuable and there are too many other quality customers out there to be too bogged down in unpleasant or abusive interactions. When you calculate the time and resources that you use to respond to, or take care of, that customer, you will see that your margins go down and supporting that sale is at a loss. Just let it go. Not every customer is for you and you need to accept that. Focus on the customers instead that are perfect for you. You know who they are already in your business when everything about the relationship feels good. Those are the people who you want in your business; they are those who you turn into raving fans which we covered in Chapter 7.

MEDIOCRITY IN EMPLOYEES

LISTEN, IF WE ARE not going to accept mediocrity from the outside, then we surely will not be allowing it from the inside!

This one is last on my list, but not least. It's the most important. Your company is only as strong as the people you hire. In a small business, hiring is scary enough as it is. I mean it's your money; your hard earned money. You have to give it away and put trust in a stranger that they are going to produce for your customers and assets the exact same way that you do. Hiring is scary, but just like vendors and services, you are better off without them than to have people in your organization giving you 46 percent instead of the 100 percent you deserve, while eating up your cash.

You're better off outsourcing parts of that position where you just get the results and save money, than letting someone come in day after day that doesn't give you 100 percent. These mediocre employees come in late, call in sick a little more than most, they have excuses for things not getting done, or they never have new ideas and shoot down ideas of others without real reason or logic. You keep them for many reasons, or maybe they come on time every day, but they don't look too interested, and they have made it obvious. You know who they are already. You sometimes make exceptions for them, or allow certain things to slide so that you can keep limping along. There is always one in each bunch.

One of the main reasons is that you have already invested in them! You sent them to training, opened your doors, let them into your home and, unfortunately, they know your secrets! It takes considerable time and resources to really invest in building quality, high-performing team members. You gave pep talks, gave them a motivational book to read, or forwarded that post from one of your favorite blogs, just hoping this is the moment that they finally turn around and get better. You joke with them every once in a while…they are like family. Let me stop you here. The employee is just like your vendor: you shouldn't, you mustn't, and you can't allow mediocrity to exist in your organization. Mediocrity on the inside of the engine leads to engine failure.

Mediocrity in employees has no doubt the greatest impact on the bottom line and growth in *any* size business. The same way that mediocrity will hurt you in serving your customers is the exact same way that mediocrity will severely stifle you in the dynamic growth in your business that you were meant to have. You must keep this in mind at all times: mediocrity is simply not a fan of big thinkers, big dreamers, or big planners. Listen, you're going to have employees who may not be on board with your new plan, new visions, or your new objectives, and you may have ones that are on board with the visions, but simply don't put in the amount of effort or care needed to achieve them. Once you start thinking bigger, dreaming bigger, being and acting bigger, the train has started to move and there are really only two options they need to hold onto. They can either prepare for the ride and be just as excited as you are about the journey ahead, or they need to get off of the train.

Four major, amazing results of letting go of small thinkers in your organization:

1. The core team will *make you stronger*. Think of it like that big piece of meat you're going to roast. You get to trim the fat. Yes, fat sometimes tastes good…but we all know it's bad for you.

2. *You'll move up faster* without that dead weight. Dead weight slows you down, it's ugly, and it doesn't add value to the final picture.

3. Most importantly, no more distractions as you're trying to weave left to right through your weekly, monthly, and quarterly figures. You and your team will *now have laser focus* toward the objective.

4. Last but not least: *you make room* in your organization for big thinking and great thinking because the limitations will no longer be in your way. As you have those discussions, you will no longer have to suffer with the interjections from small thinkers of what's not possible and what can't be done or what may seem too difficult.

While we're talking about employees and filling up the vacuum with small thinkers, let's touch on hiring awesome people.

RULE NUMBER ONE TO AWESOME HIRING

FORGET ABOUT BACKGROUND, EDUCATION and the real nitty-gritty of that resume. Personally, as a rule of thumb, I do not hire resumes. Anyone can tell me on that piece of paper that they have fourteen unique skills, know five languages, and thrive under pressure. I am not interested in a person who has memorized how to accomplish a task, or memorized the amount of steps it takes to get to a result. I'm really interested in that person who has the skill, the ability, and the will to rethink the standard and provide a solution that is an alternative to the typical path. Big thinkers are worth way more than a super-certified PhD, to a triple black-belt, six sigma director manager.

Why?

The person who's going to use the textbook is never going to have the answer that you really need to grow your business. Big thinking leads to unlimited creativity and creative solutions to business problems that produce tangible growth and bigger bottom lines.

I am convinced that only big thinkers produce substantial results.

Every dollar we spend in our small business is critical. You make a strong investment if you don't focus on the resume and experience, but instead focus on their ability to get creative in finding solutions. After all, that's what being in business is—finding a solution to a problem.

As far as I'm concerned, textbook answers and facts only make you money on Jeopardy! Innovation is what pays the bills—facts don't.

Grab a pen, and let's think through this together.

1. **Who is the small thinker on your team?**

2. What ways do they display their small thinking?

3. How does that impact your team?

4. How would things be different if they were not there?

5. Why have you kept them for so long?

6. How much do they cost you each year?

7. What are their top three functions/roles/responsibility for your company?

8. Can we get those three things done by outsourcing?

9. What will happen if you don't get rid of this person?

10. Do you have an idea for what needs to happen next?

TEN
DOES EVERYONE KNOW YOUR STORY?

"The world will never know you're
the best until you tell them."

–Tiffany Largie

How many different ways do you communicate to the world that you are an expert with amazing products or services? If your answer is one, then one is not enough. If you're only using one or two methods to communicate your value or your company's value to the world, you're operating too small. In the spirit of BUILDING THE DAMN THING, you want to use a variety of methods within the many avenues that are out there starting with, but not limited to, those that we can automate and are free.

Be willing to learn and adopt new ways of communicating your value. I feel wholeheartedly that this part of viability is left behind because of a myriad of reasons, but at the core, because the company has a presence online and the CEO doesn't.

I cannot even begin to tell you the amount of CEOs who walk into our live events or come to our office for consulting and start their journey by telling me that they are trying to keep their business and their personal life separate. In all fairness, I'm not encouraging you to share with the world what you ate for dinner last week, the new shoes you just bought, and every single little detail about your life. However, as the CEO of your company, I am asking you to entertain this concept with me: you are 100 percent the spokesperson for your company. In this book, I won't talk about being the spokesperson too much, but I will tell you that you are the expert in your field and I really want you to operate like that. Are you the expert in your field? Truth of the matter is that you sit inside of an industry, whether it's chimneys, hairstyling, house care, or even being an accountant or lawyer— it's all the same to me. You are in the midst of an industry, so you should be the expert.

In every single market there are two different types of people. There is the general practitioner and then there is the expert. I teach this concept a whole lot at our live events and to our clients around the world because this is the lesson that really changes everything. I am a huge believer that general practitioners make general practitioner money and experts make expert money. The expert in any field will alway be paid more than the general practitioner because they have positioned themselves at a higher value. As you take a moment to explore this concept, I want you to think about the last six weeks, I want you to think about the last six months, and if you've been in business long enough, I really want you to think about the last six years. Have you walked into the industry and positioned yourself as the expert in the market or just a player in the market? As a CEO, I will never run a company to be amongst my peers. I will always be in the market high enough to leave my peers amongst themselves. It has nothing to do with me belittling the people around me, but everything to do with me elevating who we are. I am very clear that my company solves a problem, and when we solve that problem, what comes after is a solution. The person who has the money in the market has the problem and it's up to us to present ourselves, our companies, and our brands in a way that makes it clear we have the solution they're looking for.

At the end of the day, no one is ever looking for anything that's average; not even close. Everyone is looking for above average. We all always want the best. As a consumer, I want the best person doing my hair, the best car in the market, the best neighborhood to live in, and as a CEO, the best employees. When I'm traveling to any given city, I'm constantly challenging what is considered the best food in the area. I want the best, and truth be told, not only do I want the best, but I am willing to pay for the best. Whatever it is that we believe is the best, we are gonna spend the money that the best has declared is the cost for the service or product. This has continued forever with no exception. I'm pretty sure that you would agree with me, no one is ever excited about having the average or run-of-the-mill solution to their problem.

We only wanna spend money one time for the solution and not have to address the problem again, which is why we spend our money on whatever we believe is the best.

Here's the tricky part about this concept though. The market won't know that your company is the best if you don't directly tell them. Who is better qualified to tell the world why your company is the best other than you? No one. You are the absolute best person in your company, no matter the size, to tell the market what problem you solve, who you solve it for, and what gives your company the right to solve it. All of this translates to answering an important question on our building journey: Why are you the best?

Two things need to sink deep before we move on. First: the world doesn't need the average version of you; it needs the best version of you. Second: the world will never know that you are the best until you tell them. Crazy thing about being a business is that you can't just tell people once; they need to be reminded literally over and over again.

Think of your favorite coffee place, favorite brand, favorite phone, really your favorite anything. You've seen an advertisement from them more than once, whether it be on the TV or some social media site. Each time the message is slightly different, but overall the same. The best of all of these belong to the richest company in the world. They are the richest company in the world indeed, but it's not by magic. That company became the richest company in the world because Steve Jobs focused on standing in front of the Apple product, the Apple story, and the Apple vision, highlighting it as a solution to a problem that the world really didn't understand at that current time. Think about this for a moment. Before we even had the iPhone, Steve Jobs made us believe that we were in trouble carrying around a BlackBerry, beeper, PDA, laptop, calculator, calendar, and anything else that we thought of as a tool to help us be more productive at life and at work. I remember working quite happily back then with my laptop, flip phone, and calculator in my bag. However, through opinion data that turned into intangible fact, he used his position as CEO and visionary to paint a better future for us all by taking heed to a solution that we didn't know we needed to a problem we didn't know we had. That is pure genius. By creating the problem in the market, he created the doubt and forced the consumer to believe that they needed to own an iPhone. Never in the history of history has there been a time where people of all races and all income brackets stood in line for hours on end waiting to give a tech company money in the sum of over $500 to hold onto a device or an item that they had never seen before. Do you remember that? Do you remember that time in 2007 when the iPhone came out and people were waiting in line till forever? Think about what I'm saying for just a second. People had never even seen the device, but yet they felt a need for it and a loss without it.

Game changer. This is the epitome of creating demand for your product or service. You know how he did it? He spent time. There were months and months of talking about the problem. The expert (a.k.a. the CEO), for the sake of our conversation, talks about the problem in the market and they use their platform and access to their platform to talk about the problem. How often do they talk about the problem? They talk about the problem as much as they possibly can, whenever they can. The CEO is the greatest poised person in the company to understand the problem, to talk about the problem, and to create the urgency in the market of how bad the problem is and how urgent it needs to be solved. The better the CEO presents this problem to the market, the easier it is for the market to consider needing the solution. Then the search is on for identifying who has a solution provided and who the expert is. Does that make sense? In the last thirty days, how many times does your company talk about the problem? More importantly, how many ways are you talking about the problem in the market? The company that focuses time on talking about the problem gets the ears of the person who is hunting for a solution online. Whenever I build anything, I'm constantly looking first for the problem to be identified, not what you do or don't do. The customer is not interested in what we do, but the problem.

One of the key things that makes an expert clear to identify in the market is content. It's almost impossible to be identified as the expert in an industry or category if there is nothing for the market to evaluate their expertise within. Right now your company should be producing content in a structured professional way consistently throughout the week, month, or a year. Taking a look back at Steve Jobs, he took to the stage and brought some of the biggest and best minds together. He stood on stage for a few days and talked about the problem. This format was consistent and it allowed him to position himself and his company as the expert in this department.

I am going to build a list of the most common reasons that companies come into our studio in Phoenix, and the ones I do each year for our brand:

- **To build a branded signature virtual event for customers and employees.**
- **To start a podcast for either the CEO or the company. (We do both.)**
- **To create a newsletter. (These are still valid and people still read them.)**
- **To write an email more than once a day. (I hand-write maybe two–five emails every week to our non purchased base.)**
- **To head into media: TV or Radio interviews.**
- **To get on a stage or speak. Yea we are taking it to the stage.**

As crazy as it sounds and as imperfect as you may feel, taking one of these and adopting it to your weekly cycle would pay dividends, elevate your brand, and give your company the positioning it deserves. There are so many other ways in today's market, but speaking is my favorite as of today. We do it ourselves for our companies, build, and then help produce each for our clients. For sure greatest impact, greatest results. These simple five will move the needle in your business a whole lot faster than you blanketing your neighborhood with postcards.

LOW-HANGING FRUIT

BASIC MARKETING MUST BE a reflex that we do each day, but it can't all be through paid traffic. Some of it must be organic. We often leave this part of our business on the table because at times it feels overwhelming or a little complicated. There is this illusion that all companies need to spend big dollars on marketing or they must devise a massive plan.

Marketing serves three key purposes in every business: to drive awareness of the product or service in the marketplace, to create trust by establishing the brand and, lastly, to produce leads that can be converted into sales, revenue, and therefore profit. The easiest way to get in front of marketing, or rather marketing efforts, in our company is to spend a little bit of time on the customer experience. Your current customers, your current customer base, and their current connections are always going to be your greatest avenue for additional cash and moving units in your business. This is literally just a moment of simply building the damn thing SMARTER.

What does the customer experience look like for your small and large customers? Is it the kind of experience that not only has them begging for more but telling all of their friends?

I've got to say, I love going into the Apple store…I don't even have to buy a product on that particular day when visiting and they literally make me feel like a million dollars. That customer experience is only magnified when I actually do buy a product—which is thankfully not such a rare occurrence—and you know what happens in return? Apple, for free, has me as a local ambassador in almost every city I visit. Every live stream we produce, and every large event that I speak or keynote on stage, I've mentioned Apple or its products. In the last twelve months alone, I have helped more than twenty people acquire an Apple product simply because I rant and rave about who they are as a partner for us. The experience is unparalleled. There is so much value in just being one of their customers.

Think about all of your favorite brands. I know what mine are. I see them, and as a consumer, no matter where I am, I trust that the product and service provided will be consistent and amazing. You and I both know that there are many different coffee options in any given city, yet somehow without fail, Starbucks dominates them all. Every last one. They are the one hundred pound gorilla in the room. You and I both know they did not create their fans because of the price. They have created their fans because of their consistency from city to city with product, service, and what I call "the customer experience." It is all about the brand. Regardless of where you are in the world, you can be confident of the consistent, quality experience you will have when you walk into the front door of a Starbucks location. They are committed to creating raving fans. I will spend my money faithfully there without question, anywhere, anytime. Do your favorite brands have the same effect on you? What effect does your brand have on your target market? On your customers?

If you are relying on referrals to produce the leads for you one by one alone, your business will burn out and you will burn out with it. Making every meeting, connection counts, and forcing it to develop as far as it can in that FIRST encounter is everything. It will save you time, heartache, and a zillion follow-ups from your company. You are only one person and can only do ONE thing at a time honestly. Getting this right is vital. As a small business owner, you wear many hats, sometimes at the same time. That's the problem; not wearing all the hats…but attempting to wear them all at the same time. No one can sustain all hats being worn at the same time.

LESSON 1: COMMUNICATION IN BUSINESS IS THE BASE OF MARKETING

YOU MAY NOT BE a one-man show—you may be a team of many—but the question remains the same: How many ways do you communicate to the world about your amazing products and/or services? I asked this before, but what I didn't ask you was: Are these ways working? Are they relevant?

There are some things in business that are optional. For example, you can be in business for years and never hire another person. You have the option to do that and depending on what kind of business you run, you can grow without it. On the other hand, marketing my friends is not one of them.

LESSON 2: MARKETING IN BUSINESS IS NOT OPTIONAL—IT'S A MUST

IF YOU ONLY HAVE one marketing avenue…it's not enough. If you only have two, it's not enough. Your customers are in so many different places today, you really need a holistic approach that can target and reach customers through several channels depending on how they receive information. Just because a business has relied on paper mail or word of mouth for years does not mean that they can ignore the necessity of emerging technologies like social media. I know we've talked about this before, so I am hoping that you can answer these questions. In order to be effective in marketing, you must know **these three things**:

1. **What do my customers want?**
2. **Why do they want it? What problem am I solving for them?**
3. **Are they clear that I have a solution for that problem? If so, where online can they head to, right now, to stumble upon me without typing in my company's website?**

We talked back in Chapter 8 about how you show up. Man, this is the absolute truth. How you show up in your marketing will either make you or break you in business. Today there are many more mediums that can market your business than there were 15 years ago. What I love most about the mediums I see today is that most are free or really inexpensive and, more importantly, they have an infinite reach. Let me just say this in black and white—if you're not focusing **at least** 50 percent of your marketing efforts on the internet, you are missing out on a huge amount of money. Just the thought of how much money you may be leaving on the table this year alone is making me sick.

I can remember a few key clients telling me that their type of business had no purpose on social media when they first started to work with our company. Just hearing it was plain old frightening. Not because I felt like they should just be on there for the sake of being there; I knew automatically, right out of the gate, how much money they were leaving on the table. Here it was: they were on the hunt for more cash flow in their business and really thought that they needed another strategy, a new tactic that they had a trailer for, and or an online funnel, when really what they needed was a presence online. They needed to be stumbleuponable. You need to be stumbleuponable. I don't care who you are, what you do, how big you are, or who your target is. Your customers are there. You are just missing them, and they are missing you.

HOW TWITTER SAVED THE DAY

THERE WAS THIS ONE time I was putting on an event in another state and the day before I had scheduled an important meeting with the committee heads. This meeting was absolutely critical to the success of the launch the next day. There were no straight flights going to the state that I needed to get to, so I perused over the options, prices, and times. I decided to go on American Airlines. I wanted to make sure that I got there on time, and more importantly, I didn't want any hiccups. So I caught a 6 A.M. flight out of Raleigh with the expectation that I would be landing at my final destination around 10:00. Somehow, American Airlines had to delay my connecting flight because they didn't have an aircraft available when I landed. I was furious! There I was, stuck in the middle of an airport, and the end was nowhere in sight. It was 8:27 in the morning and they were trying to tell me that they hoped to have a plane here by 12:15. This would put me behind by almost six hours!

My whole day shot. Absolutely unacceptable. There was no good reason like the weather or something; it was beautiful outside. There just weren't enough planes available that day.

Frustrated, I got on the airport Wi-Fi and looked hard to find a phone number or email for customer service. I called a handful of numbers and got nowhere fast. Losing ground, I turned to Twitter. Yes, Twitter. I sent a simple tweet that went like this:

> *I chose AA for the fact that I knew they would get me to my destination on time and now I am going to miss my entire event!*

Within two minutes, I got a response on Twitter asking me for my flight number. Needless to say, they made me a fan, kept me as a future customer, and have gained more money from me since.

Again, go back to the three questions I asked you earlier in this chapter:

1. **What do my customers want?**
2. **Why do they want it? What problem am I solving for them?**
3. **Are they clear that I have a solution for that problem?**

ELEVEN
LEADS

"If money doesn't come to you, you go to it."

–Tiffany Largie

Your business should have three to five ways of creating leads that are independent of you. Leads are the lifeline of your business. In the previous chapter we talked about your "more" in terms of getting in front of your marketing, which was just wrapping your arms around the basics. Now I'm going to match that with wrapping your arms around the most solid foundation of your business...sales. Sales are the blood that run through the veins of your business and they affect every partner, every customer, every team member, and everything that is even remotely tied to this business that you're running. I'm even going to go so far as to say that not only is it tied to your business, but the sales in the company you run today are directly tied to the life you live today. Your lifestyle, your ability to do something, and your reason for not being able to do another thing—they are all one in the same.

The truth of the matter is that if I can get you to just entertain your sales game as a department that belongs to the CEO, and for that matter will forever belong to the CEO, then the course of your entire company will change. I don't care if five years from now you hire a VP of sales and they are the person in charge of running the sales game for you, they will never be able to replace you and they will never be as impactful as you can be on the bottom line of your business. That sales number and/or sales goal has to come from you because it has to be tied to the vision that you are putting forth into the world. When you think of sales, I want us to directly correlate it with the term "revenue goals."

We should be selling the value of our company on a regular basis. There are three different types of revenue that every company should be focusing on, should be selling into, and should have a set way of acquiring that lead and moving that transaction along.

THE ACTIVE REVENUE BUCKET

THIS IS THE MOST common revenue bucket that companies have in place today. It means that we actively provide a product or service and in return we are paid dollars. With this particular bucket we can do so many things. This is where we begin to hire people to fulfill. In general, when you think about sales, hiring is of the utmost importance, but for the success of this specific bucket, hiring is critical. In theory, if my company needed certain insertions of cash, or it needed to expand, grow, or scale in another way, as tempting as it would be to hire more people who could sell our products and services, I actually would not hire anymore salespeople. First, I would hire more people to support the fulfillment side. If worst comes to worst, I myself can always push for the sale, but what I can't do, and what I don't have time for, is fulfilling the purchases. One of the biggest mistakes that companies make when they're looking for more is they say, "Oh! I'm just going to hire more salespeople, because if there were more salespeople, we would sell more products." However, the truth is that in the art of scaling, selling more products is great, but if we don't have enough people to fulfill those orders, we're in trouble, and we actually cannot expand. Truth be told, the CEO is still the greatest sales person that there ever could be for your company and your brand, so we kind of have that covered. Active revenue is how you pay for your overhead operations and a lot of your fixed costs such as your lease or mortgage, your fixed assets like coffee machines, leases for cars, and the fixed costs inside of the tools that your company depends on to run each and every day.

Most businesses do this in the form of one-time transactions, and it's actually very good, but you want to know what you're great at? Active income paid to the company in the form of recurring revenue, which I referred to as "R.O.R". "R.O.R" in any company creates a foundation for you and I to confidently collect dollars in the form of active income, but it may not be actively done at that second. For example, if you have a client who you provide plumbing services for, they call your company, so you dispatch someone, and they fix it. If there is a plumbing issue and they were there for five hours at $100 an hour, they now owe your company 500 bucks. The better way to support this customer is to offer them an annual maintenance plan for a fixed rate, or a monthly plan for $5.99 that lasts 60 months. Then when your team comes out, they get twenty percent off of any service that you perform for them. The beauty of this is that, over the course of five years, the customer is going to spend $359.40 in addition to one or two, maybe even three, other services that you offer. Now, you don't have to use five years exactly, but think about it. That customer is going to live in that house for at least five years. You can change the math and make it three years, or two years, but it's not gonna change the fact that you now block in the next couple of sales from that customer versus them having the opportunity to head back to the phonebook or internet searching for one of your competitors, and choosing them the next time.

Most of the time, when it comes to sales, a customer may not choose us, not because we didn't do a good job; they don't choose us because we are not top of the line, we're a little bit out of sight, and we don't have any connection to them at this moment. That maintenance plan that they are spending five dollars a month on may not feel like a lot, but I'm going to tell you from experience that it forces the customer to be sticky in your relationship, and you want them to stick. When they stick, that means that, when the next problem arises, they automatically know where the solution is and you don't need to spend any more dollars on your budget or in your budget to acquire that lead. Does this make sense?

I like to use active income to pay for the things that are going to be fixed costs in our company and take care of our overhead. When we collect that payment in smaller chunks over a period of time, versus looking for all of the dollars from that customer the first time, we engage them and that is where the magic happens. It means that we could have a really bad month, but respectively, we still have a set fixed amount of dollars that come in. It allows our company to pay our bills over and over again. I cannot tell you how many times I have used this or had this in place and it saved the day. It's a must for every CEO to make sure that they have in place before moving on to the next bucket of revenue.

THE LEVERAGED REVENUE BUCKET

I LOVE LEVERAGED INCOME and this form of revenue is absolutely number two. It's number two because it allows us to take our same products and services and set up a different strategy inside of a company. Instead of selling to one person, we take the one product and we focus our efforts on selling to many at one time. Inserting this into your business year allows you to easily and fluidly double, triple, and quadruple not only your revenue, but your profitability. One of the other cool things about leverage income is that you get to focus on a different product for leveraged income and put yourself in the driver's seat for making sure that your company is moving all of your different products and services. The idea is not necessarily to move all of your products and services every single month; it is actually to make sure that in a calendar year they all get to be part of the solution bucket for people seeking answers from your industry. Your products and services become known because of the amount or the kind of results they are producing for clients. Leveraged income or revenue means that you are taking one product and selling it to many.

THE MODEL THAT WORKS

EVERY SINGLE QUARTER IN my hardware/software business, products did a live event in my office. It would take me a little bit of time every single quarter to get my arms around, but for the 10–20 hours of preparation we made hundreds of thousands of dollars in a single day. I would do the work once and develop a boss strategy for inviting targeted people in our community into our office at a very specific time, one-by-one. Each quarter, I focus on a different vertical market quarter. One I typically focused on was IT directors of the community colleges, healthcare, and K-12 school boards. I flipping loved these events. I would teach some form of specific application combining hardware and software into their industry, and I would bring in a machine to show them. It would cost me anywhere from $500-$1000 to have experts teach at the event and we would patch them in from wherever they were in the world. Through a unique commitment process, the attendees would show up to their free event and we would be able to teach to many people the same exact thing just one time. It allowed us to go deeper, faster, and quicker in our sales cycle. Within 30–60 days, we were in the midst of a new contract and we had moved hundreds of thousands of dollars.

Inserting this once-a-quarter into my business model allowed me the confidence and the strategic positioning to ensure that we had a consistent place to move our products and services, but not just any products and services. For us it was a production unit that we focused on. That would be any machine that was valued at $50,000 or more in revenue when we sold it. We knew that within the audience of 15 people, we were for sure going to get 2–4 of them to say yes to an offer that had some combination of products and services. Do you have a product that fits into this price bracket? Or something you would feel confident in labeling HIGH TICKET? And if you don't have a product that fits into this number, do you have the type of customer that might buy, or prospective customer who might pay for 40 of the units that you are selling? If I could get you to find a product that, if you sell maybe less than 15, you get to 50K, you win. Your company MUST have some form of high-ticket offer or product available for you to have rocket years.

Can you think of a customer profile that, if they bought from you in the next ninety days, would equal a $50,000 sale? That's the criteria in which I want you to think about this; that's a criteria I want you to apply to your leveraged income application sale. You could definitely duplicate in a short period of time. If you don't have an office or a showroom like we did, you could rent out a local hotel conference room, a local showroom, or community center.

One time, we had too many people who confirmed they were coming, so we rented out a local college print shop and ran the event there. It worked like a charm. We had the same exact impact and we created a win for Livingstone College for allowing us to use their space for the day. They got the opportunity to show off their amazing print shop, to talk about their college, to possibly position themselves to take on outside print jobs from the local market, and to create a revenue stream for the college that wasn't there before. The concept or key here is that you talk to many people and more than one person has the ability to buy at that moment. I did this in the form of a live event, but you could also produce this same exact thing in the form of a virtual event. You could 100 percent take the virtual event model, produce it once a quarter, and have the same impact on your annual numbers with ease. Connecting with the local market in a unique way is important, and giving your company a place to show how awesome they are is the objective.

Whether you are inviting people one by one, running local ads in your city, or just sending out an email to your current customer base, the gathering of people is an event. Teaching once on that day, along with making one offer, is all you need to get a percentage of them to say yes on the spot to whatever the next step is. This is where the magic happens on your profit and loss statement.

You make sure that in addition to the sales transactions, your company has a solid, secure way to showcase your expertise to many people at one time, therefore more than one person can make a decision at once about your company's solution and then, as a result, you move more than one product at a time.

THE ADDED BONUS OF ONE TO MANY

ONE OF THE ADDED bonuses to this strategy is that the whole company gets the opportunity to be involved in it, which is one of the things I love the most. It allows us to have this camaraderie kind of peace where we are working on something all together respectively at the same time. We're each taking a piece of the pie in terms of tasks and executing with finesse. We come together to celebrate a massive win and then move on to duplicating it and figuring out how we make it better. Building a platform for yourself to showcase your expertise and your company's awesomeness in front of multiple people is one of the fastest ways to elevate your status in any market. It's where you take the rightful place that you deserve in your industry.

People who are seen teaching in their industry are often thought of as the leaders in their industry. It is an easy way for you to walk into "more" out of what you are doing already.

BONUS: HOW WE GOT THEM TO REGISTER
AND CONFIRM

WE AVERAGED A 95 PERCENT show-up rate! This is one of my favorite parts. I love that I get to share with you exactly how we did it. I wish that after all these years I could confirm the rumors we used to hear from manufacturers when they would watch us execute these events. Apparently we were casting spells, using tactics to brainwash these people, and that's the only reason they showed up consistently, but it couldn't be further from the truth.

We just committed them emotionally to what they said that they were going to do, so that way they took the first step, because if they took the first step, then chances are they were going to meet us at the second step. Therefore, they will be willing to walk with us to steps 34 and 35 in the sales process.

I would have my guys head over to the specific community college and leave some form of an envelope, a letter, or an invitation that talked about the event on one side of the invitation only and then it had a Panera bread menu on the back. It was amazing. The Panera bread menu on the back was so good because they would then talk to the IT Director and talk to the secretary and have the IT Director choose exactly what they wanted on the menu; they would have them write on the actual invitation. My team was trained to emphasize that the event was 100 percent free and we were going to allow them to not only choose what they wanted from Panera bread, because everybody loves Panera bread, but we were also going to let them customize their order. No mayo, extra cheese on toasted bread, you name it. The customization forced the IT Director to feel emotionally connected to what was going to be happening at the event. After all, we are holding their personal, custom order from Panera bread that we took so long to craft just for them. Because it wasn't generic, and we made it just for them, they then felt obligated to make sure that they came through and attended.

The day before, I would have my administrator call each person and confirm and let them know that we had put in their order already, we couldn't wait to see them, and then repeat that we have the sandwich coming in, plus their no mayonnaise, no lettuce, no pickles customizations. We would tell them that we ordered them an extra cookie, because it was my favorite, then we asked them at the same time to confirm what time they would be walking in.

Even though we knew that the event started at 12 o'clock, we wanted them to get connected to the action that they were taking. We wanted them to visualize what time they were leaving their office, hopping in their car, driving over, and getting out so that they could adjust what was already on their calendar if need be and that we became the priority. This strategy worked quarter after quarter. We whipped out these events using the exact same strategy, changing nothing. Panera bread was awesome and provided custom boxes with the clients' name on it through their catering department absolutely free and for roughly $10 a seat. I got 10–20 of the biggest names in our city to show up, allowing us to be amazing, and to moves a sales cycle farther along. This typically would not have happened.

This is an instant way for you and your entire team in this sales world to become more. The entire thing may have cost me $200 in food and possibly $2000 in equipment, however you could minus the equipment completely and just use the things that you have in your office already. You could stimulate them virtually, you could play videos, you could ask experts to speak virtually, and showcase this on the big TV. There are so many different ways, and if you can't figure out how to quite get it done for your company, please reach out to our team and let us help you. It is one of my favorite strategies to use in the market in a clean, clear way to establish yourself as an expert and have an easy way for your whole team to make money together.

In business, I use leverage to pay for new hires for growth and to force us to stretch like when we built our studio or acquiring more locations, like when we built a studio, or when we think about acquiring more locations. We need some technical expertise training for a company. Literally and truly, leveraged income is what I used to pay for the additional things outside of our fixed costs in our business. It gives me a way to dream, to plan, and to stretch. So, for example, if my production manager says to me, "Man, we really would be in a great place if we could buy such and such camera." I go, "Great. How much is that camera?" When they tell me the cost, it allows me to go, "Awesome, this is going to come from my leverage income." Doing this allows us to hear goals, and allows us to speak more strategically as we're planning ahead.

There was a time in which we wanted to buy a building for a little over $2 million, so I looked at the year ahead and I said, "OK great. I'll top off our fixed costs. How much will we need for a down payment?" Because if we said, "Hey, we really need $300,000 in cash," then I knew right out of the gate that if we created an "X" type of event and invited "X" type of people, we could move "X" amount of products between quarters 1 and 4 to do it.

There was a good chance that if the right opportunity came to our door, we were going to be ready for it. It's one thing to dream about being able to do this, and another for us to have a secure method in our current business model to make it happen. We know how to easily build a road map to MORE.

Leverage income is how I pay for all the extras in business, new hires, training, needs for our studio, and just growth in general. Areas we want to stretch in. Our team, right now, at this very moment, is trying to get me to consider creating our own branded tour bus! I'll be looking at our leveraged income opps to figure out if and when it is possible.

How can you take this next upcoming quarter, or maybe even the one after that, and implement something like this? Gathering people, showcasing your expertise and your knowledge, and selling your products and services to many people does not have to be in the form of an all-day event; it could literally be 90 minutes.

THE PASSIVE REVENUE BUCKET

WHEN BUSINESS OWNERS ARE looking to up their cash game, they often turn here first thinking that passive income comes right after active income. Wrong move. It doesn't. Passive income is third. The reason why it's third is because it is something that is slow grown. It does not happen overnight and 100 percent has a buildup. Once the buildup happens, it's amazing; but it takes time and has to be intentional.

PASSIVE REVENUE TYPE ONE

THE FIRST TYPE OF passive income that every company should have is in the form of intellectual property acquisition. When I mean by that is the CEO or the company is sitting on a level of knowledge on how to do either a whole thing, or a particular thing, and even though your company sells that service or product to do it for the customer, I don't want you to underestimate the fact that the customer or people who cannot get to you because they live in another city, state, or country want to acquire the same knowledge. The way that we do that is we put it into a format where we create it once, then we set up a way for them to acquire it online over and over again. We only touch it once when we are building it. Some of my millionaire friends describe this best as "digital real estate." You create one product, one time, and that product sells over and over again without you having to touch it at all.

If someone wanted to, right now, at this moment of the time, wanted to buy something from your company, even small, could they? Could they give you the money right now without anyone in your company having to interact, follow up with, or talk to them on the phone? If they can't right now, they should be able to. It is an easy, low-hanging fruit.

Let's say you are a small business selling vacuums or repairing vacuum cleaners. I'm going to use this example because it'll appeal or apply to you whether you have products or services. People come into your shop all the time to get their vacuum cleaner repaired for $60 once a year, and they buy a new vacuum cleaner every three to six years. The fact of the matter is, that if that company simply had a little e-Book, or tiny pamphlet, that said how to care for your vacuum cleaner at home so it lasts longer for $19.99, I bet half of your customers would buy it. Now, let's move away from your local customers and let's move into the group of people who are scouring the internet right this very moment trying to figure out how to get more out of their vacuum cleaner and they live 2,000 miles away from your shop. With that digital real estate, you can literally service that customer right from where you are. Although you can't sell them your active income or active revenue products, you can surely sell them one of your passive income products, because now you're already positioning yourself as the expert and they're going to trust you no matter where you are. That person doesn't care whether or not you're in their backyard; they care only if you're going to solve their problem.

Here are a few samples of things your company could and possibly should have right now:

- An audio tape explaining how the customer could implement a DIY version.
- A video of the customer being walked through a DIY version.
- A workbook of the customer walking through a DIY version.
- A course for the customer.
- A kit that has all three audio workbooks and a video.
- A checklist.
- A guide.
- A case study.
- An eBook.
- A replay of a workshop or a master class that you have done already that has instant-replay ability.
- A book like this one.

Honestly, the possibilities are endless. You would be surprised who is paying for information at this exact moment right around you. It doesn't even have to be the whole thing that you teach them; it could just be one component of it.

Do the math with me. If your company sold ten items a week simply by people searching on the internet, we could have a "buy" button on your website, or some form of a landing page for that situation, and they would be able to obtain the digital real estate that you have sitting out there (a.k.a. digital product). Then we could set up a handful of automated emails afterwards to nurture and take care of them the same way you would if you had planned a phone call. If we did ten of these a week at $100, that is $1,000 a week, $4,000 a month, and $48,000 a year! That right there would pay for the new assistant that you need right now. Or it could become the base salary for the Marketing Director you've dreamed of hiring. And if it's not that, it'll pay for the team trip that you've envisioned taking your company on for years now. All I know is that these things aren't just going to pay for something awesome; they're going to pay for something that you need, and for me that's paying for the fun.

The second way that you can embrace this concept is by getting people to pay you for recommending their products and services in the form of being an affiliate for the software and hardware that you are already using. We collect thousands of dollars every single year simply by recommending the products that we believe in to our customers and clients. But we're not just recommending the products that we believe in, we're recommending the products that we use on a regular basis and that we know well. I am going to be talking about them at some point, somewhere. If it's not on our BUILD THE DAMN THING podcast, it's going to be on stage, and if it's not from the stage, it's working one-on-one with our communities. So if I'm going to talk about that item, it only makes sense for the manufacturer to pay us commissions on our ability to drive traffic to their offers. Right now, you have a handful of vendors who you're spending money with that are knee-deep in being able to provide an awesome product or service to the people you love the most, and you're missing out on being paid. We have an entire section of our company for this, but more importantly, for me it became an intentional focus a couple years ago. Some companies do this and pay commissions in the form of an:

- **Affiliate program**
- **Partner program**
- **Ambassador program**

Truth is, you could create your own, but that would be a leveraged outcome, not passive. We are in the passive section, but I just had to plug this in while I was thinking about it so you knew that it is 100 percent an option for you too.

BRAND AMBASSADORS (PARTNERSHIP)

BRAND AMBASSADORS CAN BE the game-changer in your small business. I just love this method because it's something you can put into play immediately, and more importantly, it's really about creativity.

You can't expand any more than where you are. Resources are limited at this point. You give everything 100 percent, but that's it; you're maxed. You love your brand, you love your products and services, and believe in them completely. You're out there promoting your brand day in and day out, building your business…but what if, every day, there were more people talking to other people and companies about your amazing brand, product, or services?

In our case, we turned the Brand Ambassadors into almost "un-employees" or sales reps for us. Instead of one person talking about your business, you have five people talking about your business. Let's say five Brand Ambassadors talk to 25 people each day. We've just created reach.

Now you are able to extend beyond your own personal reach without much more effort. Your new ambassadors are going to have a customer base that is different from yours. This method is a total win. You instantly get access to a database other than your own, in addition to a set of potential prospects that are warm and already in love with your brand. It's perfect. If you choose the right company to partner with, you'll gain a few key things: loyalty, quality customers, and strength in your own offering.

There are two sure ways to create and compensate brand ambassadors quickly and efficiently.

Here is a step-by-step list of securing your company's FIRST Brand Ambassador in the next 30 days:

1. *Identify* **a complementary business. Do some research. They already have a customer base, and more importantly, a different reach than you have. I would narrow it down to three industries that are complementary to your services.**

2. *Buy one* **of their products or services; become a customer. Before you engage, this will allow you to evaluate their process and connect with**

integrity. It will help you make sure that they are the perfect fit and someone you want a part of your team.

3. *Schedule* a meeting. If they are local, ask the owner out for coffee or lunch. They must be clear on the value that providing your services will do for their customers, and more importantly, they are going to be looking to see if you are providing stellar customer service with an awesome product.

All right, so once you do this and set up the meeting, naturally they are going to want you to answer a key question: What's in it for them?

If you are dealing with a small company, the value is really tied to revenue; smaller entities are always looking for ways to add to their bottom line. They have limited resources, so the ability to sell an additional product without adding staff is enticing.

If the company is larger, money still plays a role here, but reach, brand, and market share may be a little more valuable. I would approach both scenarios with one of these two ways.

Wholesale it. The first option asks you to create a wholesale price for your product or service. Now, don't be afraid of this unless you're wondering if there's enough money left over after the cost to offer a small discount. If you are operating on such low margins to start with that there is barely any money left over, you're gonna have a growth problem as it is. We may need to halt here and take time to look at your actual pricing and product. Be the big thinker and use the wholesale method to allow the Ambassador to sell the product along with their own products or services on your behalf. You don't have to hire that salesperson, nor do you have to be the only one each day talking about your product.

You can't grow in any direction without margins or a rather healthy profit in your business to support growth. With healthy margins, you can offer your partner a wholesale price that they can then mark up to their customers directly.

Break off a piece. This is a little bit different than wholesaling it. In this scenario, you take a small part of the margin and offer it almost as a commission. You have to be careful with this method and be clear on your margins before you use it. Using this method ensures you don't lose money through the partnership and protects your profit. Now there are two ways to do this.

METHOD 1

I SELL WIDGETS FOR $100 and my profit is $40 per widget. I offer you 10 percent of the total cost (keep my actual profit private). You make $10 for each one that we sell together. In this scenario, both parties win. You are writing a check in the form of a commission for each item sold monthly. If you are selling products or services that have a low price point possibly under $100, this may be a good method to try. If you are selling higher end services or products, then possibly you will need what's coming up next.

METHOD 2

I'M SELLING THIS PRODUCT for $100,000. If you offer them a percentage of 10 percent like in **Method 1,** then you could over-commit yourself, and more importantly, give more money than is deserved. Personally, I would not be willing to give away $10,000 on my sale with the commission rate of 10 percent. Instead of a percentage of the sale, you offer a fixed amount as a form of commission. So instead of the commission rate being based on the revenue or sale price, we base it on product type. So, together we sell product "A" and I give you $100 flat, product "B" $250, and so on and so forth. This keeps your profits safe, and more importantly, you don't put yourself into a position of over-committing. Again, both parties win with this method.

WHO REFERRED YOU?

MANY YEARS AGO I HAD a friend who moved into an apartment complex that we all knew he could barely afford. I asked him how he planned to pay for that apartment for the next twelve months and he told me that he had a plan. Apparently this apartment had a referral program for its residents. The program was simple: "If you refer someone to become your neighbor after they pay the first month's rent, we will give you fifty percent off of your next month's rent. Help us and we will help you!"

Now keep in mind that this apartment complex had other methods of generating leads, but even with all of those options, they understood the power of their happy residents providing that word of mouth to vouch for their product.

One month after he moved in, he went to work. He talked to everyone he knew and sometimes to people he didn't know! After all, this was South Florida and his rent was $1,400 a month for that one bedroom.

Before long, he had moved in a total of nine people, and for three-quarters of that year, his rent was 50 percent off! This was another win-win for all parties involved. The customer liked the product and had no problem telling people about it. I am sure, however, the gracious incentive helped a little.

TWELVE
SUPERSIZE IT, PLEASE!

"When life gives you lemons, cut them open, take the seeds,
and plant trees...but when those lemons grow, sell them all."

–TIFFANY LARGIE

WHEN I GOT OUT of my car and parked, I was clear on two things. One: I wanted a value meal...I was crazy hungry. Two: I was pretty clear on how much I was going to spend on it because I had had it before. As I stood there, and the cashier took my order, she then asked me if I wanted to "supersize it." Pure brilliance.

There I am, the consumer, starving and ready to eat. I'm ready to spend roughly seven dollars to get a complete meal. In my mind, I'll be satisfied, until that question comes up. Supersize it? Forty-nine cents? Sure. What's the additional 49 cents to my seven dollars I am already spending? At the time it was insignificant. After all, I am super hungry, so I'll get a larger fry and a bigger soda. The consumer won...right?

This method of getting more from me was simply BRILLIANT. You don't have to like McDonalds in order to appreciate this example, but you do have to understand it. They needed to add revenue to their bottom line and made a decision at that time to not produce a new product. They simply offered a little more of something they were already providing. They gave the customer the illusion that there was great value in the additional product. This is perceived value. The customer feels like they are getting way more value for the money than they are spending. By asking that simple question at the end of every order, McDonald's added millions to their bottom line with little effort.

If your core offering stays intact, what can you offer to your customer that would not be laborious or expensive to create, but adds tons of value? Maybe it's something you already have?

Let's try a similar concept and look at it in another light.

Think of revenue-building like a pizza shop. I have an absolute favorite pizza shop in Miami, Florida, which for now I'll refer to as The Pizza Place. In my eyes, they make the tastiest pizzas ever!

As a customer, when I come in, nine out of ten times, I'm strictly looking for their core offering—a cheese pizza. I could stop there, spend my $10.99 and just get a pizza: cheese, sauce, and dough; but they don't let me. They always proceed to ask me if I want any toppings with my pizza. I look up and see additional items that I can add for a small price—ham, meatballs, pepperoni, olives, the list goes on and on. My mouth is watering just thinking about it.

All of the toppings cost $1.99.

Now here's the reality: no one walks into The Pizza Place and just grabs a bowl of pepperonis for $1.99. Same scenario as McDonald's. I am already spending $10.99; what's an additional $1.99 for a topping? As the consumer, this is insignificant to me, but for The Pizza Place, this adds huge dollars to the shop's bottom line. For McDonald's, the $.49 offering couldn't stand on its own. Nor could the pepperonis. They only make sense when added to the core offering.

So if I order a pizza with green peppers and pepperoni, I am spending $14.97 versus the $10.99 that we started with. That's an instant increase of over 35 percent from the same customer!

THE CORE OFFER

EVERY SINGLE COMPANY SHOULD have a core offer. JUST ONE. This is the item in the market that they are known for, and more importantly, this is the item in the market that any consumer can acquire, right now, with ease. An offer differs drastically from products and services because an offer is a combination of your dope services and amazing products that come together to become a **core** offer. Sometimes for our clients we refer to it as their "signature offer." In developing a core offer, you don't in any way have to choose the items that have the highest price. That's not the goal at all. The goal is to come up with an offer that has a handful of key products, experiences, or services included with it for a fixed price that allows your customer, or prospective customer, to solve the acute problem that they have and the pressure of the problems they have right along with the acuteness.

The reason why a core offer is so important is because it allows the expert in the market to really focus on their expertise. That means that the core offer is presented to the market as a solution and as a response to a problem in the world. It helps to position and establish them so that they become known for something. Everything else that they sell is a lateral or a supportive product to their core solution. In the previous chapter, when I talked about leverage income, I actually didn't focus on a different product from the norm, I doubled down on what we had become known for in the market. Even though we sold and represented all of Xerox's manufacturing line, we became known in the market for production. We were after anyone who was either putting out a large volume or was printing a high-level, high-quality application. I stuck to the products in which I knew that Xerox was the absolute best and had very little competition. Their regular printers and normal copiers were fantastic, and in my opinion they were a cut above the rest in all categories. However, there would always be something from another competitor that would highlight a feature that was similar and it forced me to provide education in order to get the sale to convert.

Hey, I'm not here to say that education is not good, but after a while of constantly educating the market, it gets exhausting. I really wanted to be out of the game of constantly having to educate our audience and constantly having to try new creative angles to differentiate ourself in the market. That is when I decided to focus on their higher-end products. Though more expensive and with fewer customers who had the potential to buy that product, I knew that, in business, it was the area in which Xerox Corporation had very few competitors that could produce the same quality. I also allowed myself to focus on what had the best quality in the market and not so much of what would be the most cost-effective amongst our audience. When creating your core offer, it's tempting to want to have the best and most-creative price. That is not my style, and it'll never be my style.

I have never had an interest in being the most economical choice in the market. Instead, I have always had an interest in being the most valuable choice in the market. This driving force is a whole new level of excellence. When you commit to the price that you believe is best associated with the value of your offer, you let go of the audience in the market who buys on price and disregards the value brought to the table. I just feel that if they are looking FIRST for the cheaper option, I should let them. They are not my type of customer. I know my value.

The person who's always trying to find the cheapest price for what I was offering totally missed the fact that our company came along with the value of the product itself. My team and myself were part of every single sale and what you were buying was not just the widget and the item that would land in your office. You were also buying our many years of expertise, or accessibility, and our knowledge around helping you get the most out of the investment you've just made. That is the truth of an offer— understanding all of the value that you bring to the table for your customer.

PLEASE CHARGE FOR THE KNOWLEDGE

EVERY SINGLE TIME SOMEONE buys something from your company, they're not just buying the item, nor are they just buying a service. They are buying the many years of your expertise, knowledge, failures, wins, and you getting to that point. It is so important that I highlight this, because if I allow you to think that the value that you have to the market is wrapped up in your product or service, then I fail. Your true value to the market is inside of the knowledge and expertise that you have and bring to the table while you provide a product or service. Your expertise, care, concern, love, and commitment to excellence and mastery comes with it. I didn't just sell machines; I knew exactly how that customer could make more money in their print shop if they acquired our equipment. Actually, if they acquired just new equipment on a whole. Spending so many years in the industry allowed me the confidence to quickly tell customers what would and wouldn't work. The second that I did that, not only did I up my own value, but I added a tremendous amount of dollars to that customer's bottom line by helping them do whatever it is that they do better. I have already gone through all the trials and errors so that they don't have to. They get to save money by getting to the results faster, all because they've had my company be a part of the sale.

I want you to think of your company holding the same amount of weight, the same amount of value—no less. Every time you sell to the market, you are offering them your many years of experience and sometimes it's just the two or three sentences worth of information that changes everything for the company. With Xerox, even though we did not manufacture the product, the second that we supplied the product, we won an opportunity. We did not manufacture the product, but our knowledge on how to best use the product, how to make more money with the product, and how to create a better impact with the product for the customer—that knowledge was priceless. It's priceless because your customer gets to consume your YEARS of knowledge in a super-short period of time, making life easier for them and the result they want closer.

Today, there are amazing humans who fly in from all over the world to our office and studio in Phoenix, Arizona. They do so because they are looking for help in development with a product or service, or they're looking to reorganize their business. In the form of a VIP day, a production weekend, or a story boot-camp, we help them figure that out very quickly. We are the experts and have mastered this process in our own world over and over again.

Now, every so often I take on a client personally who needs a custom approach, and in our *Shadow CEO Program,* I can help them. It is where I'm going to help them get through their life as a CEO and their life as a human, at the exact same time, so that we scale their life and scale their business at the same time. I help them build a stronger company in all of the departments and bring their team, sales process, and marketing focus back on track. Sometimes I have to overhaul the brand while I am there. Whatever it is that gets them to being the positioned experts in the market, I implement it. At times it requires me to go on-site to their business.

When I walk in through the door, I'm not carrying a bunch of books, guides, or PowerPoint presentations to walk through with them. Fixing that business is a master process that resides within me. I know how to turn this company around and help this CEO build the kind of life that they have always wanted.

We charge for that knowledge because, in a matter of moments, hours, days, and a few weeks, they get to acquire all of the knowledge and shortcuts that are in me that comes from 20 years' experience in making millions of dollars, losing millions of dollars, and learning tough lessons. That shortcut is priceless, but we have to put a price to it. The key here is to price your time and be clear on the outcome for your customer. I know for a client that working privately with me produces millions of dollars for them.

One of my very first clients, and now one of my best friends, Mark Stoner, was doing a little under four million dollars when he became a client.

He runs a chimney company in Nashville, Tennessee. He became a client because I positioned myself as the expert at that time within a service-based business. Now keep in mind, this was well before I had a brand like DO THE DAMN THING behind me or any real team members, but it didn't change the fact that my knowledge and expertise came first and foremost to the table.

As I began to walk through one part of his company, my expertise led me into other departments. I really had to own my own confidence on what I knew and trust myself to share with him the shortcuts that I knew because of my own experience in running a service-based business while trying to balance my life and up my marketing sales game. I figured it all out through the years and brought my businesses more money.

He hired me at first just to build a service program for one of his departments, but what he got was a whole lot more. He got my knowledge and many years of lessons from doing this type of work in all the businesses I had run before. People I had hired built programs that taught shared knowledge, but he acquired the shortcut…a direct implementation of my expertise and guidance. In under five years, Mark's company went from being a 3.9 million dollar company to a 10 million dollar company. Today, he owns seven more companies, he has more time, more freedom, and more everything as a CEO than he ever did before. My knowledge was the catalyst for change in all of his departments and helped him to fast-track the result he really wanted. Today, Mark's company, Ashbusters, has made the Inc. 5000 list twice! He just purchased the largest powder-coating company in the U.S. in his industry.

We can't just share our knowledge for free, because if we share our knowledge for free, in addition to providing great products and services, we miss out on becoming a more profitable entity, and in return, providing better products and services to the market. The more profitable you are, the stronger your company is in your industry.

You can hire the best people, you can pay for better resources and training, and you can acquire tools that you need versus being trapped by the tools that you can afford based on your current budget. Possibility is super key in building your core, offering additional dollars in one of the prime areas. I see CEOs just leave ridiculous amounts of money on the table every-single-day, every-single-year, and it literally drives me crazy from the inside knowing that they are giving away knowledge to their customer and not quantifying it. Even if you don't actually charge your customer for the knowledge, you should be in front of them quantifying the fact that you gave them that knowledge in the first place and acknowledging for yourself, your team, and everybody else that that knowledge comes with a price. My knowledge took a lot of tears, a lot of lost time with my children, and a lot of hitting my head wrong on absolutely everything. These companies that I run, any company that I run in the future, and my ability to share that knowledge with someone else will absolutely come with a price because it's valuable and it's the kind of understanding that is not usually found in a book.

Experience in the market or in the world is the only thing that becomes fact. It is the item in the world that will move the objectives faster, because someone else has already been through it, so they know the ropes, they know how to navigate it, and they know how to get there in the best shape, in less time, spending less dollars, with way less wear and tear on the team and the CEOs themselves.

With every core offer, there should absolutely be a supersized opportunity to go with it. There should be an opportunity for that customer to get deeper with you to get more help or simply to have more.

If the pizza place can find a way to up their dollars on the same core offerings, you can also increase your profits on your offers. Start with these questions:

1. What is your core offering?
2. Do you have a supersized option in your business? Think in terms of package deals (buy 1, get one free; buy 2, get 1 half off)
3. Do you have a second?
4. Do you have another?
5. What could we price it for?
6. Who would benefit from this add-on the most?
7. Why would it be of value to them?
8. What language could we use to introduce it?
9. Would we offer it on paper?
10. Would we offer it before the sale?
11. What about after the sale?

THIRTEEN
THE KICK-OFF PERIOD

*"They need transparency from us. They need the vision
casted from us. They need to see themselves and where
you're going and how you're moving forward."*

–TIFFANY LARGIE

YOU HAVE ALL THE pieces that you need to BUILD THE DAMN THING now. I am sure somewhere inside of you is a myriad of thoughts around which part comes first, how to begin, and where to begin. In my life and in my businesses, I really enjoy bringing all of the ideas, thoughts, and concepts into a central location. This makes it stupidly easy to distribute and unbelievably easy to delegate, plan, schedule, evaluate, and brainstorm. This is how I make sure it happens. I'm going to break down the two most important steps that I would do next.

First and foremost, I would absolutely schedule time with my team, my executive team if possible, and I would take an entire day or two to bring this book to what I'm going to call a planning meeting department-by-department. I would create a Massive Action list on what you need to do, and instead of listing all the potential things you could do, I would limit it to about five areas of impact in each department. The thing is, when you're doing this you really can't be in a place that you're comfortable with or somewhere that you work all the time. You really truly need to change your environment. Changing your environment is absolutely critical to you beginning the journey of developing fresh new ideas and a fresh perspective on how you're going to BUILD THE DAMN THING NOW. Your environment will dictate so much on your ability to create, be creative, and execute.

If you do not have the funds or time to book a trip to a city or a state across the country, or across the world for that matter, and you cannot make it to our office in Phoenix, Arizona where we can help you with a VIP strategy session where we map with you in person, I want you to consider going somewhere new, but local in your city. This might look like booking yourself an overnight hotel or weekend or an Airbnb in one of the weeks coming up. This is a time when you are alone from Friday to Sunday. You are doing nothing but dreaming out loud, building a page-by-page action map, and more importantly, making really hard decisions about what you will no longer tolerate so that way you can get to the next level. One thing I absolutely love is bringing a big white sticky pad with a bunch of markers so that I can write on the paper, tear it off quickly, and stick it to the wall instantly. Hours later I end up surrounded by a road map.

You have everything you need to build a dope road map. One that you can execute and also one that you can share with other people so that they can help you execute.

The second thing that I would do either right after or in conjunction is schedule a kickoff. I absolutely love kickoffs! They are a fun, creative way to centralize your team, vendors, contractors, and all people involved into a common conversation. It is then you can divulge your new ideas, thoughts, and perspectives. Moreover, you get the buy-in that you need.

A kickoff is something that large Fortune 500 companies do all the time. They fly their people into some fancy hotel and they just talk about what's happening. I adopted this same principle maybe two decades ago because I wanted to build for where I was going, not for where I was. Even though I wasn't a Fortune 500 company myself, it didn't change the fact that I needed to respect myself like I was a Fortune 500 corporation and I needed the people who worked for me to treat and see it as such with the utmost respect.

This philosophy has paid dividends ten times over the last two decades. My kickoffs are always two days. The first day is for me to deliver some form of the State of the Union, the second day is for me to walk through ideas and thoughts and then to open up some brainstorming sessions so that I can get the feedback from people who know our brand and Company best. They give me an idea as to where they are or where we're going next, what that looks like, and how we can make it happen. I know for a fact that these two days allow all of our ideas to be on the table, but also gives me the ability to get the emotional connection I need from the people who support me…my team.

They need transparency from us. They need the vision casted from us. They need to see themselves and where you're going and how you're moving forward. They need to not only see the vision, but be able to place their own impact and vision alongside it for their own growth.

Kickoffs give the sexiest ways to do this because they are seamless and you really don't need a lot of resources to make them happen. No matter how large your company is, you should be having at least two kickoffs every year. One during the first half of the year, and one during the second half. Really and truly, no matter what that one right at the beginning is, it needs to be somewhere between January and February. This is critical, because it sets the tone for the year. Every single year my team roughly goes away during November, December, and January for what we call planning meetings, and then that's followed by some form of a kickoff. We have another planning meeting during the middle of the year that we use as a kickoff which allows me the time to get deep in training to make our people stronger and to cast the vision out further. One of the greatest things that have come out of a brainstorming session that we have had together as a team is this tour bus. I would have never have imagined that we'd be the kind of company to have a tour bus, but lo and behold. We have mock-ups in our office now and have already identified where we would place a logo. We've even gone so far as to design what this place would be, how many people it would sleep, and how we could use marketing. We are well down the path in executing our very own tour bus.

It's going to happen. That level of dreaming wouldn't even have been remotely possible if it hadn't been for our team coming together, me sharing and casting the vision, and them inputting and dreaming out loud.

I don't care how far away your dates are in the future, please set them on the calendar now!

1. **You need to schedule time to go alone so you can plan for two days. If you don't know where to go or how to do that, reach out to us. We might have an open date in the office for a VIP day and it would be best for you to do it with us.**

2. **Please schedule your kickoff. You need at least four weeks into the future for you to have and hold your kickoff.**

DON'T DO IT ALONE

ONE OF THE BIGGEST lessons I learned on my journey to multiple seven figures and building a global brand was that, if I was going to go, I could not execute the whole damn thing on my own. I told myself a million things. It was easier this way; it would be too complicated to explain it to other people…I've even gone as far as to say that they just wouldn't understand. What I learned was that it wasn't really about my ability to delegate as much as it was for me to make sure I had the right person or people in place and that I would do whatever it took to make sure that they were clear on the vision. Scaling your vision is one of the hardest things you'll do as a CEO, but it's one of the most rewarding things that you can do. Not only do you build a platform big enough for other people to stand on, but you build a platform strong enough for your own dreams. The very first step to this is you scheduling the time and making it real. Literally, that's the very first step. I would go right back through this book with a highlighter pen and take notes. Use it as a workbook lab manual, and if you ever feel lost, you can reach out to us or you can attend a live event with it. This book will always be the key to some form of a discounted ticket, complimentary ticket or above, because now that you've gone through this DO THE DAMN THING process and you're on your way to building the damn thing once and for all, we know that you're family. We can trust you and we know where your heart is. You wouldn't have gotten this far on this journey with me if our hearts weren't aligned. You would have closed the book, thrown it away, or talked shit about me to someone you know for the next couple of weeks once you had hit Chapter 4.

It's tempting to want to ask your spouse, family, or friends their opinions on what you should do and how you should do it. I found out a long time ago that their opinion was irrelevant if they didn't run a business and or a life the size of yours to be. They had great opinions, but no facts or data to support it. Which meant that as grateful as I could be, they could not point me in the right direction or give the emotional support that I needed.

I am extremely grateful. Grateful that you gave me your time, and grateful that you chose me to serve you. I can't wait to watch you win; I can't wait to watch you #**DOTHEDAMNTHING**. Become more and conquer you so the best version can take center stage.

FOURTEEN
YOU'VE GOT THIS!

"The world doesn't need the average version of you;
it needs the best version of you."

–Tiffany Largie

Sweet Jesus, omg, you did it! What a journey we have been on together, and even though it's felt long, the truth of the matter is that it was short. In such a short time, you've accomplished so much, but I know that you are just getting started. You're on your way to building a life that you love with a business to match. You've got this. I wouldn't have spent the time writing this book if I didn't believe it was possible and didn't believe in the purpose that you are here to fulfill. I promised for a long time that I was going to head around the world to help every single human reach their maximum potential before I leave this earth. You might be asking yourself, "Well, what's in it for me?" And transparently I will tell you that I have the luxury of planting a seed in you that I know will grow beyond my reach. You're going to touch people in this life that I will never get to and therefore my work and my promise to God is being fulfilled through you. Real talk: there are so many problems on this planet, and as crazy as it sounds, I don't believe for a second that the world's problems were created to exist without solutions. I believe everything has a solution.

Racism, sex trafficking, the foster care system, our judicial system, homelessness and hunger on this planet…I don't believe in any capacity that they are problems that will be solved by politicians and awesome nonprofits. I believe that politicians and nonprofit organizations have their place in the solution, but they don't lead it; they can't lead it. They can't lead it because these problems are all economics at the end of the day, and last time I checked economics and all things related to commerce really are in the hands of business owners. I believe with every fiber in my body that business owners and entrepreneurs are holding the answers to the world's problems. They are the only thinkers who naturally have the capacity to process both at the same time. They have the capacity in their heart to be empathetic and sympathetic at the same time and to balance that out with a needed challenger to the problem related to dollars and cents.

This is exactly why I made a decision to start this mission. I wanted to focus on tapping into the world's untapped potential. I wanted to find you— the person who just gets me. The person I don't have to explain myself one hundred and fifty times to as to why I do what I do. You feel me in some regard and you feel my heart. What I need more than anything is more people like you on the frontline. More people like you who have the capacity to care more about people outside of your circle. You have the capacity to build; see, I'm like you who crave more in this life.

SO WHAT'S HAPPENING NEXT? DECISION TIME

So WHAT'S NEXT? What's going to change? What's the first step to take in DOING THE DAMN THING? What's the first step in you BUILDING THE DAMN THING NOW? Real talk: I don't want you to wait anymore to make it happen—life is too damn short for you to wait any longer to have the money you want, the family you long for, the home lifestyle you crave, a brand that makes you excited for the type of customers you relish working with and, more importantly, the catalyst for this all is the kind of business you've always dreamed of. Don't underestimate the power of now and don't underestimate the momentum of now. There's this crazy idea that you should take your time and slowly walk into your changes. I have to challenge that narrative. I actually don't believe it.

Ninety days before publishing this book, I was suddenly rushed to the emergency room in the middle of the night, where I had emergency surgery within two hours of arrival. According to that surgeon, if I had arrived there just minutes later, I might have died. No, I didn't understand. I felt completely unprepared, and because of how quickly I was taken to the hospital, not a single person knew where I was. I was alone. I was reminded of the power of now. I may have been tempted to wait until I was ready mentally for the surgery, until we could notify my team members, family, and friends. But the urgency of me making a decision to trust what was in front of me all happened in the now. After spending almost two weeks in the hospital by myself in the midst of what we now know together as a pandemic and covid, I knew that there was no room for me waiting to do the damn thing in my own life. Not only did I need to get back to building the damn thing, but I needed to build the damn thing now. I also needed to build the damn thing stronger.

As I went to rehab and learned to walk all over again and found a way to have some form of an interest in food I felt, or rather, I allowed myself to bask in the urgency of me getting all this shit done. Getting this shit done is the most important part of the whole game because if I die, and I don't get it don; I'm not coming back. You get it? Once you die, you leave. We're not coming back, which means that we have to take all of our nails as if it's our last. As I wrap up my thoughts in this journey, this book is an example of me making a decision to build the damn thing now. It is an example of me starting what I finished, and more importantly it is a recommitment from me to you to push the limits of what is possible by other people.

I remind myself that just because my lowest standard is someone else's highest standard doesn't change the fact that it's my standard. Someone else's maximum capacity might be at a million, but I know that my maximum capacity starts out at a billion. I know that today. That level of knowledge, the truth of me focusing on myself, and not being too concerned about what other people are doing is the most important part of this entire journey. Not paying attention to people to my left or my right, not comparing myself about what I am and I am not, but rather being committed to just doing the damn thing every mother-effing day. I can't just do the damn thing though and wake up every day and walk around wildly. I literally need to be holding onto my map for every single step of the way so that I don't waste any time. Because again, I don't have time to waste and frankly neither do you. Both of us are running out of time. Do you hear me? This is real. We are running out of time and we need to move faster. My urgency for you to become more now is a result of me wanting you to build the damn thing now. Whatever it is. Whatever part of your life or your business that you have been waiting for. The right time to be perfect, to be happier, and for your time or cash flow to flow stronger is now. Nothing else matters. The only thing that really matters right now is your decision.

If you made a decision not to decide then you've made a choice as well. The toughest part about that is that that choice is not what you want. I don't want you to leave yourself in the cycle of managing other people's insecurities, making your moves based on what you're tolerating. Living in an environment, a house, a city, or a state that really doesn't inspire you to be your best self. I know that now at the other end of my business game twenty years in these trenches and these business streets. I'm going to tell you that taking care of myself first has been the most important part of the whole puzzle and often before I got to this level, it was the one thing I left absolutely till last. I was building a shit-ton of things in my life, but I wasn't the center or first. I wasn't included in the things I was working on. They were to benefit everyone else first. What about me? I was working way too hard to be the last recipient of my hard work. Somehow, I decided it was a good idea to put myself last and everyone else before me, though I was the one who needed strength to keep up all the things I built for everyone else?! Something about this made no sense. Do you feel me here?

I really want you to consider what I'm about to tell you because I actually need you to hear me and hear me clearly. You can no longer take the leftovers. I don't care how much money is not in your business right now. I don't care how you feel like you should be further along on your journey according to your age, race, color or any of the above, but what I do know is that what you have is yourself. You are the greatest tool that ever was to solve all of the problems that ever will be in front of you. Your decision to embrace the map that we've just built together is pure fire and I'm waiting for you to execute it. All of it. If you feel like in any paucity that you just need more help and you're like, "I love this map," "I need a little bit of help," or "I need to be part of a community," or you even just like, "I need someone who I can whisper in their ears and they can give me a surefire way to take the next step," let us know and reach out to us. We are here, we will always be here. Do The Damn Thing Nation embraces you to help guide you. We are not perfect, but we are real and honest and we will embrace you with our story.

- **NO LONGER will you drive around in circles in your business!**
- **NO LONGER will you allow mediocrity from vendors!**
- **NO LONGER will you ask a friend to help you out with a favor!**
- **NO LONGER will you allow yourself to be a victim of profitless sales!**
- **NO LONGER will you let your competitors steal your potential customers!**
- **NO LONGER will you keep "John" who only fogs up a mirror on your team!**
- **NO LONGER will you run to the grocery store with that hole in your shirt!**
- **NO LONGER will you be a victim of small thinking!**

I am so excited for you...I really am. I believe in you. I believe in the business you've started and the dream that's unfinished. But around the corner. Truth is, I know that you are so much closer than you think.

Here are some options for you:

1. Connect with Tiffany on Facebook, Twitter, and Google+ instantly. We should be connected everywhere; I absolutely want to continue the conversation.
   - www.dtdtnation.com
   - www.strappedhustle.com
   - www.twitter.com/tiffanylargie
   - www.instagram.com/tiffanylargie
   - www.youtube.com/tiffanylargie
   - Just about everywhere: @tiffanylargie

2. Go here to check what I did on three key things that you can use to build your bottom: www.dtdtnation.com/buildthedamnthing. Yep! You have a clear plan, and if you come to a live event we will make sure you get direct feedback and live coaching.

3. You get a complimentary ticket with proof of purchase included with this book to a live event. Please go to www.dtdtnation.com and find out what events are happening this year and send an email to hello@tiffanylargie.com to claim your ticket with proof. This offer will never expire, as long as I am alive. It will be to ONE of our annual events, either DTDT LIVE or the equivalent. I literally cannot wait to see you in person.

4. I personally work with only a select number of companies around the globe each year outside of the DTDT programs. I am THE SHADOW CEO. Maybe your company needs help with their company's story, marketing, and sales process and CEO's vision-mapping. I am a turnaround CEO today. If it's your sales team or your senior level executives, I've got you. The whole picture. No more DOING THE DAMN THING in pieces. If you want to drastically take your game to the next level, know there is another level for YOU, and MORE that you are capable of, and you don't know how to BUILD THE DAMN THING on your own, this is the right step for you. There is an application

on the www.dtdtnation.com/buildthedamnthing page. If you don't find it, tell me what's going on directly at tiffany@tiffanylargie.com.

5. Need Tiffany to speak and dazzle your audience on a stage at your next event? Reach out to her at: hello@tiffanylargie.com.